For all our material comfor
are increasingly fearful, rest
yet we seem strangely reluc
about who we might really be, and whether anyone really
understands, or even if we have any value at all. Rory
Shiner and Peter Orr both possess powerful minds and
outstanding communication skills, and for those who
recognize that there must be more, this book sets out the
biblical case for truth, meaning and hope in a fresh and
compelling fashion.

The Hon John Anderson AO FTSE
Former Deputy Prime Minister of Australia

In a world that is often battling to find purpose and build
self-worth in the midst of unpredictability and change,
The World Next Door is a chance to pause and reconsider
the framework through which you see life. Rory and Peter
invite us to see the bigger picture of life outside of our own
personal bubbles, and the reality that we are meant for
more... and part of more than we realize. They beautifully
unpack the Christian faith through the Apostles' Creed in
a real-life way, and compel us to consider the life that God
offers us through Jesus as they bring depth and clarity to
each aspect.

I pray that many who read this book will have their eyes
and hearts opened to the truths offered by the Christian
faith.

Debbie Flood
Team GB Olympic silver medallist

Interesting. Personal. Challenging. These are some of the words I would use to describe *The World Next Door*. In a world that has forgotten the truth about God, we need to hear it in a way that makes sense. By explaining the basics of Christianity, Rory and Peter invite us to learn the most important things of all.

Peter Jensen
Former Anglican Archbishop of Sydney

The World Next Door is a refreshing engagement with philosophy, books, film and personal experience to explain what the Christian faith is all about. Intriguingly set within the framework of the oldest and most widespread Christian creed, the book introduces us not to what we might have expected—the flawed institutional church—but to the God who created the universe, and to his Son, Jesus of Nazareth, who entered our messy life to rescue us mostly from ourselves. It is, in many ways, a love story. This is not a book full of trite one-liners. Instead, it sets out the kind of thoughtful, respectful arguments that its readers deserve.

Anne Robinson AM
Founder and Partner at Prolegis Lawyers
Co-author of *Driven by Purpose: Charities That Make a Difference*

This little book is sheer genius. Its lively, bracing exposition of the 'basics' of Christian faith is engaging, surprising and delightful. Rory Shiner and Peter Orr write with affection and respect for their readers—especially those who are 'sceptical', as they thoughtfully unfold the compelling beauty and deep significance of the things that Christians hold to be true. Their enthusiasm for the subject rolls off every page. *The World Next Door* is relentlessly contemporary in re-introducing to a new generation one of Christianity's ancient statements of belief. Buy one for yourself and buy three to give away.

Kanishka Raffel
Anglican Archbishop of Sydney

The World Next Door

A short guide to the Christian faith

Rory Shiner
AND **Peter Orr**

SYDNEY · YOUNGSTOWN

Matthias Media
(St Matthias Press Ltd ACN 067 558 365)
Email: info@matthiasmedia.com.au
Internet: www.matthiasmedia.com.au
Please visit our website for current postal and telephone contact information.

Matthias Media (USA)
Email: sales@matthiasmedia.com
Internet: www.matthiasmedia.com
Please visit our website for current postal and telephone contact information.

ISBN 978 1 925424 72 0

Cover design by Annesa Fung.
Typesetting by Lankshear Design.

Acknowledgements

Peter and I would like to thank the following people for their help and feedback on this book: Rachael Barr, Charlotte Butler, Sarah Doyle, Luke Jackson, Steph Judd, Megan Lo Surdo, Mikey Lynch, Stephen McAlpine, and Matt Pluke. Thank you to Geoff Robson, our wonderful editor and *sunergos* in the Lord. And thank you also to Andrew Moody at The Gospel Coalition Australia, where earlier forms of some of this material got their first run.

Dedications

Rory

For my godchildren: Kaitlin, Jonah, Lachlan, Josie,
Nell, Thomas, Otis, Remy, and Zali.
This is what I would have taught you if I were better
at being a godparent.

Peter

For Noel Purdy: Thank you for helping me understand
all of this for the first time.

Contents

I believe—the reason for this book

This book is our best shot at commending the Christian message to our friends. It's driven by the universal human instinct to increase the joy of finding a good thing by sharing it with others. We both think we've found a good thing—the best thing—in finding God through Jesus. We want to share it.

I (Rory) work as a pastor of a church in Perth, Western Australia. A large part of that role involves talking about Jesus to people who are secular or from religions other than Christianity. Truth be told, that's probably my favourite part of the job. Peter teaches the New Testament at a Theological College in Sydney. Part of his job involves keeping abreast of the latest scholarship, including all the sceptical approaches that claim to have disproved this, that, or the other in the Bible. So that's handy.

If anything in particular has prodded us to work together, it is our strangely symmetrical upbringings. I was brought up in a deeply religious family, but was sent to a very secular, progressive state school where I was one of a tiny handful of Christians. Peter, on the other hand, grew up doing what was then a rare thing in Northern Ireland—*not* going to church. We are both roughly the same age, and so while Peter was getting teased at school for being the only atheist in the village, I was having my Christian faith held up to (mainly good-natured) ridicule. For the quote under my photograph in the school yearbook, my classmates ascribed "Something religious"; Peter, meanwhile, acquired the nickname 'Pagan Pete'. For both of us, the secular alternative to Christian faith has always been part of the air we breathe.

The book was largely written during the COVID-19 pandemic of 2020-2021. There's nothing like a pandemic to remind us of our mortality and frailty. There have been signs, at least at the time of writing, of a new interest in spiritual matters. Google searches for 'prayer', for example, went up by 50% during the early phases of the crisis.[1] That must mean something.

Before we go any further, a brief mention of three other books might help to frame where we think this one fits.

Karl Barth (1886-1962) was a Swiss theologian, and a leader in the Confessing Church, a (shamefully small) group of Christian leaders who perceived the evil of Hitler's regime and refused to submit to its demands. Just after the end of the war, in 1947, Barth returned to Bonn, where he gave a series of lectures on the Apostles' Creed. These lectures eventually became a book called *Dogmatics in Outline*. Europe was in ruins. The landscape was scarred by the violence of war. Barth wanted to offer new hope from the ancient streams of the Christian Faith.

From 1941 until 1944, CS Lewis, the great Oxford don, author of the Narnia series, and a man once described as the best-read man in England, gave a series of lectures for the BBC on the Christian faith. These were later published as his now-famous book *Mere Christianity*. War was again the context against which Lewis was invited to commend the Christian message to the British people.

Peacetime and prosperity give us the luxury of squabbling over secondary matters. Effective health care and extended lifespans allow us to ignore the certainty of our own death. But wartime and pandemics tend to concentrate the mind. Certainly, our minds have been drawn again to the central truths of our faith, just as our hearts have been drawn to friends who have not yet considered the claims of Jesus. With Karl Barth, we think the best hope for the future in an uncertain present is the ancient faith of Christianity, as expressed in the stout words of the creed. And with Lewis, we think the task of commending that faith to those who do not subscribe to it is exciting, and urgent.

Karl Barth was a theological giant. Lewis's *Mere Christianity* was an instant classic. We make no such claim for what follows. But inasmuch as both Barth and Lewis were making an earnest plea to a secularizing culture in the midst of a global crisis, we write in the same spirit.

The third and final book to help orient you to this one is less well known. It is a book to which this book's title is an allusion—James Sire's *The Universe Next Door*. Published in 1976, the book is a guide to the beliefs, imaginations, thought patterns, and practices of the person next door, who might be an atheist, Muslim, Buddhist, or Hindu. As the title indicates, if we could see into the mind of the person next door whose belief is not our own, we would find not just a few propositions on which we disagreed, such as "God exists", "demons are real", or "abortion is permissible". Rather, we'd find a whole worldview—a way of seeing the world, indeed a 'universe'—in which those propositions find their coherence and meaning.

Sire wrote for Christians to help explain to them the "universe next door". He wanted them to think more generously, more expansively, and more holistically about their neighbours' beliefs. Our purpose here is to return the favour. We want to invite you into the world, the universe, that is the Christian faith.

What follows is roughly shaped around the Apostles' Creed, the most universally accepted summary of the Christian faith. It is associated with baptism and the entry of new converts into the faith.[a] We figure the creed will keep us on the straight and narrow, tethering us to an account of the faith that is briskly orthodox and historically grounded—the sort of *mere* Christianity Lewis spoke about.

The creed also allows us to take you in and show you around a bit, rather than just standing at the door and talking about what's on the other side. Christianity's explanatory power, bracing beauty, and sheer otherness are some of the best things about it. It ends up making our modern, secular, materialistic Western view of life look a bit, well, dull. There are all sorts of good reasons to become a Christian, some of them very serious. But one of the more surprising reasons is that being a Christian is actually really interesting and, in its own way, fun.

---

a   Baptism, practised by Christians in various forms for the last 2,000 years, is a symbolic washing with water, representing the cleansing, the forgiveness of sins, and the new life that Jesus offers.

The Apostles' Creed

I believe in God, the Father Almighty,
    creator of heaven and earth.

I believe in Jesus Christ, his only Son, our Lord,
    who was conceived by the Holy Spirit
    and born of the virgin Mary.
    He suffered under Pontius Pilate,
    was crucified, died, and was buried;
    he descended into hell.
    On the third day he rose again from the dead.
    He ascended into heaven
    and is seated at the right hand of God the Father
        Almighty.
    From there he will come to judge the living and the
        dead.

I believe in the Holy Spirit,
    the holy catholic church,
    the communion of saints,
    the forgiveness of sins,
    the resurrection of the body,
    and the life everlasting. Amen.

Part 1: God

I believe in God, the Father Almighty, creator of heaven and earth.

1

But first, demons

Jesus was an exorcist. He once cast a legion of demons out of a man and into a herd of pigs. They ran off a cliff and into the ocean and were drowned. True story.

Most Christian books addressed to modern, scientifically-inclined Westerners don't begin here. The average secular person is unprepared to take such stories seriously. And evangelists have plenty of other material to work with. Who knows? It's even possible the average modern Christian finds these stories faintly embarrassing.

But I propose we start exactly here. Consider it training at altitude. If you're still with us after the demon-and-pigs story, the rest is going to feel pretty sane.

Jesus was many things. He was a preacher, a healer, a storyteller, and a prophet. According to Christians, he is the saviour of the world, the presence of God with us, and God's appointed ruler of the universe.

He was also an exorcist.

Jesus did battle with demons. A lot. In the grand sweep of the Bible, that's unusual. Contrary to popular opinion, the Bible is not wall-to-wall supernaturalism. Vast swathes of the Bible are about historical, this-worldly events. Many of its places and characters can be cross-checked on the historical record.

But then there's Jesus. Despite the Old Testament accounting for about three quarters of the Bible[b] and more than two thousand years of history, the first recorded biblical exorcism is by Jesus. Demons, relatively shy and hidden in the first thirty-nine books of the Bible, are suddenly active, prominent, and anything but shy when it comes to Jesus. Why?

To understand this, we need a map. A map of the unseen world.

At one level, the Gospels (the four New Testament biographies of Jesus) are about our world. Jesus did not live in a time-out-of-mind, in a dreamtime, or in a mythical prehistory. He lived between 4 BC and AD 30, in places such as Galilee and Jerusalem, under rulers such as Augustus and Tiberius, and encountered historical figures such as Herod Antipas and Pontius Pilate. Jesus' world was our world.

But in the Bible, our world is not the only world. What we can see with our eyes is not all there is. And, just as the activities of the criminal underworld occasionally interrupt civilian life (the execution of Mob boss Crazy Joe Gallo in a crowded seafood restaurant in Manhattan on 7 April 1972, for example), the spiritual underworld occasionally interrupts our earthly life.

b 'The Bible' is, in fact, a 66-book collection—more of a library than a book. It contains two sections: the larger and longer first section is what Christians call The Old Testament. It tells the story of God's dealings with the nation of Israel. The second, much shorter, section is called The New Testament, which is about Jesus and his followers. When we refer to a Bible book we will cite the name of the book, then the chapter, and then the relevant verses. This way you can easily check the reference, either by typing it into Google, or locating it in a physical Bible. So, for example, a quote from the Gospel of Mark, chapter five and sentence number two, will appear as "Mark 5:2".

The Bible writers map this as a kind of triple-decker universe. In the New Testament, the apostle Paul says that "at the name of Jesus every knee should bow, in heaven and on earth and under the earth" (Philippians 2:10). There are the three decks: (1) in heaven; (2) on earth; and (3) under the earth.

Heaven (the top layer) is God's space. Heaven is where (in one sense) God 'is'. It's where his angels are. It's the place from where God rules. You hear this in the prayer Jesus taught his disciples, called "The Lord's Prayer" (or sometimes, "The 'Our Father'"):

...your kingdom come,
your will be done
on earth as it is in heaven.

Heaven is where God's will is done. The prayer is a request to make earth more like heaven, to bring God's rule (his "kingdom") from there to here. The Nyoongar version of The Lord's Prayer captures the idea perfectly: "Your word will come here and be boss on our ground as you do in your holy and sacred home".[c] Heaven is God's holy and sacred home.

Earth, the second layer, is our home, our ground. In biblical thinking, we are very much from around here. The first human's name, Adam, means 'the dust man' or 'the earthling'. We are made of the soil and depend upon it for our lives. Humans are not wayward angels, lost aliens, or eternal souls temporarily encased in meat-suits. We

c The Nyoongar people are the Indigenous people of south-west Western Australia, where I live.

are earthlings. We were made, says the Bible, to be God's image-bearers in this space. We were put here to be a picture to the earth of what God's rule is like in heaven.

Finally, at the third layer, we have the underworld.

In common understanding, there is a place called 'hell'—the place of punishment for the enemies of God. True, that's part of the picture. But in the biblical map, it's part of a wider reality often called 'Sheol' or 'Hades', 'the place of the dead', or simply 'below the earth'.

It's not hard to think how this language came into use. Humans, when alive, live on the earth. When our loved ones die, we bury them. We put them under the earth. And so, 'under the earth' becomes associated with 'where the dead are'.

There you have the biblical triple-decker universe mud-map. The heavens, the earth, and under the earth. God's place, our place, and the place of the dead. That's the map we need.

One more important note: things got badly messed up.

As part of humanity's rebellion against our creator (of which much more below), the whole world has become dis-ordered, dis-integrated, messed up. Things are not as they ought to be, and things are not *where* they ought to be. Just as under conditions of climate change we are starting to find polar bears in odd places, or fish migrating out of their usual regions, or bumblebees dying where they used to thrive, so too, in a world in rebellion against its creator, one of the symptoms is finding spiritual creatures a long way from home.

Creatures such as demons.

In the story where I began, Jesus and his disciples travel

by boat to a place called the Gerasenes. They arrive at a cemetery and there encounter a man who has been possessed by what the Gospel writer calls "an unclean spirit" (Mark 5:2, ESV).

Now, let's apply our 'map' to this scene. Where is the man? Among the tombs of the dead. What has possessed him? An unclean spirit. What's going on here? It would seem a spirit from the underworld has found its way into our world. There's been a breach of the border in our triple-decker universe.

Under control of this spirit, the man's life has been rendered chaotic. No-one is strong enough to subdue him. Night and day among the tombs he cries out. He cuts himself with stones. Isolated from his community, unable to be constrained, he is both overpowering and overpowered—a threat to others and to himself.

What is the nature of the force that has assumed control of this man's life? Demons are popularly assumed to be fallen angels. That would certainly be the majority opinion. But I have an alternative for your consideration. I think they might be ghosts—by which I mean the spirits of dead people.

Three reasons.

First, ghosts are a thing in the Bible (see, for example, the story of the prophet Samuel's ghost in 1 Samuel 28).

Second, notice the words the Gospels use: "an unclean spirit" or "a demon". A spirit (one guesses) cannot literally be "unclean". What would the dirt attach itself to? But uncleanness can also be moral and religious. In the Old Testament, association with death warrants an automatic red card into the unclean category. And the spirits here *are* associated with the dead. They live, after all, in a cemetery.

They are also called "demons". In the literature of the time, that word is sometimes used for minor deities or fallen angels. But the word is also used for the spirits of the dead. It is used especially for those spirits of the dead who continue to make their presence felt upon the earth. Often, these are spirits who have unfinished business on earth. Like Hamlet's father, their death has embedded an unacknowledged injustice, or their burial was irregular, or their cause was unheeded in life. Estranged from their bodies, they now wander the earth looking for a host. Dislocated from their proper home "under the earth", they now search for a temporary home in a physical place or another's body. In the Gospels, demons are always looking for a home.

Third, ghosts are a ubiquitous feature of human culture. Almost every human society has an account of spirits of the dead making their presence felt in our world. Who am I to dismiss so much human testimony?[d]

Jesus versus the demons

Whatever demons are, they are from the underworld, the realm Jesus is confronting. Chapter 5 of Mark's Gospel records one such moment of confrontation. When a

d   At least, that's what I (Rory) think they are. For the argument in favour, see P Bolt, *Living with the Underworld*, Matthias Media, 2007. I don't think my co-author is persuaded, and he's an actual biblical scholar, so factor that into your assessment. Whatever they are, they're definitely creatures from another realm, which is the main thing we need to know about them.

demon-possessed man sees Jesus from a distance, he runs and falls on his knees in front of him and shouts at the top of his voice, "What do you want with me, Jesus, Son of the Most High God? In God's name don't torture me!" (Mark 5:6-7).

Notice the concern to 'name' Jesus. Demons have excellent theology. If you ever find yourself sitting a theology exam, quoting New Testament demons is a sure-fire path to a High Distinction. They never put a foot wrong. Here, the spirit names Jesus with precision: "Son of the Most High God." Snap.

But the demon is doing more than trying to spruik his theological prowess. He is seeking to control Jesus by naming him. In the world of the occult, the world of magic and sorcery, names have power. From traditional cultures to the classical world, through to He Who Must Not Be Named in *Harry Potter*, names are a source of power. To name correctly is to release or to exert power.

Remember the quote before, from the apostle Paul? "At the *name* of Jesus every knee shall bow, in heaven and on earth and under the earth..." Names matter.

In this context, Jesus' reply is vaguely comical. He says to the spirit, "What is your name?"

Jesus won't play the sorcerer's game. He responds to the attempt to 'name' him with aplomb. "What's your name?" is Jesus' nonchalant response. (His name, it turns out, is "Legion", for "we are many".) The spirits, now cowering before Jesus, beg Jesus to find a new home for them. Homelessness—being away from the underworld in which they belong, or the bodies they once inhabited—is the fear that drives them. If this man can no longer be our host, then what?

"Send us among the pigs", they beg Jesus.

Jesus consents and sends them there. And the pigs, now possessed by the spirits, rush headlong into the lake and are drowned. In the ancient world's map, such bodies of water (lakes, seas, oceans) are seen as a kind of portal to the underworld, pores through which AWOL spirits can return to the world from which they have escaped.

When Jesus arrived, he found a dangerous man and a legion of unclean spirits escaped from below the earth. By the end of the story, the man is seated and in his right mind, and the spirits have returned to the place from which they came. Jesus is putting things back into order: in heaven, and on earth, and under the earth.

Demons and the Christian faith

Starting a book for secular, 21st-century people with demons might look like an own goal or an unforced error. The Bible is not particularly focused on demons, angels, the heavens, or what's under the earth. For the most part, the lens is firmly focused on our world.

So why start here?

Francis Schaeffer, a Christian thinker from the mid-20th century, apparently used to give his first talk on angels when addressing university students. When asked why, he explained that when he spoke about God and sin, people heard him to be speaking about morality. But when he spoke about angels, people understood he was speaking about spiritual truths. About a bigger reality, about transcendent truths.

That's what we want to talk about, too. In the chapters that follow, the questions of morality and the good life will find their place against a background of bigger realities: God, Jesus, the Holy Spirit, together with the heavenly hosts of angels, and the underworld armies of the un-dead. Rather than give you arguments for the existence of such worlds, we'd prefer to simply invite you in, boots and all. On the way through, we'll offer some explanations here, some defences there. But the real explanatory power of Christianity can only be experienced by indwelling it. The Christian faith is less like an object in the world, whose existence is accepted by some and denied by others, and more like a pair of glasses through which you look at the rest of life, the universe, and everything. We think it makes sense. But more than that, we think it makes sense of everything else. Magnificently so.

No hell below us, above us only sky

In the modern West, we live in what philosophers call an "immanent frame". We have framed out transcendent realities, such as God and angels, or the Good, the True, and the Beautiful. We may or may not believe in such things. The point is we have 'framed' them out, much as a picture frame includes the painting and excludes everything else. We have put them to one side and decided to get on with life as if they were not there. Perhaps they are; perhaps they aren't? The point is we don't need them in the picture to get on with things. No hell below us, above us only sky.

The result? In modernity, we have more freedom than we did before. More prosperity. More opportunities to invent and reinvent who we are. We have been freed from any sense of purpose, of *telos* or proper ends. We don't look beyond ourselves for meaning. We generate meaning from within. The army used to encourage enrolments "For King and Country". Don't think about yourself; think about something bigger. Today, the army invites us to 'be your best self'. Our identities are fluid and malleable. We no longer look outside ourselves for fixed points from which meaning can be established; we look inside, and seek to discover the authentic self within. The most trustworthy voice is the inner voice. Spoiler alert for every Disney film since the early 1990s: You can be who you want to be. The hero lies within you.

This view of the world hides a dark underbelly. If who you are or what you become is a product of your free choices, then who you are is also your fault. You and you alone bear the entire weight of your own self-realization, your own meaning-making. No-one can help you in the search for the authentic you. You're on your own, buddy. We can remove some constraints, but beyond that? The best we can do is shrug and say: "Well, if that's what you've chosen, then good for you". We have freedom, prosperity, and agency. We also have some of the highest suicide rates in the world, we are beset by crippling anxiety, and we experience *acedia* (listlessness, purposelessness) on a scale unknown to the ancients.

Modernity has put a burden on humanity that we don't

have the capacity to bear. We simply were not made to generate our own meaning. We were made to be part of something bigger. Something cosmic.

The triple-decker universe spoke to this. It put human life in a bigger frame. It included a more complex set of assumptions and options by which to make sense of human choice, of guilt and suffering, of meaning and home. It had something to say when we hit up against the limits of our powers, the curtailments of our creatureliness. It confronted us with real responsibility for our sin, while relieving us of the impossible and oppressive responsibility of supplying our own meaning. Where modernity looks down over thick-rimmed reading glasses and says, "Well, maybe if you'd tried harder...", the ancient, transcendent view was more compassionate; expansive. It had room for us to understand ourselves as simultaneously victims and perpetrators, noble and base, free and enslaved, responsible and in need of rescue.

That's the Christian claim, at least. Which is what the rest of this book is about.

2

God

Christians believe in God. If you become a Christian, so will you. Perhaps you already do?

Many believe in God prior to becoming Christians. Some believe in a different god, and Christian faith changes which god they believe in. Still others have a hazy, ill-defined grasp of some sort of god, to which Jesus brings clarity.

But for many in the Western world today, to become a Christian entails a move from atheism (the belief that there is no God) or agnosticism (not knowing whether there is a God or not) to theism (belief that there is a God).

God and the gods

On Stephen Colbert's *The Late Show*, an interview with British comedian Ricky Gervais turned to the topic of God. Colbert (a committed Catholic) wanted to know more about Gervais's atheism. On Colbert's declaration he believed in God, Gervais answered:

> But there are 3,000 to choose from! ...So, basically, you deny one less God than I do. You don't believe in 2,999 gods. And I don't believe in just one more.[2]

The joke illuminates a common misunderstanding. It confuses the idea of 'God' on the one hand with 'the gods' on the other. When Christians (or, for that matter, Aristotle, Maimonides, Abu Ali Sina, Immanuel Kant, or Russell Brand) say the word 'God', they mean something qualitatively different from 'the gods'. Gervais's joke is based on a category error. The gods are beings; God is Being itself.

Let me explain.

At one level, Gervais is right. Humans have, for almost all of their history, believed in 'gods'. They have believed their universe is populated by powerful, active, non-human agents. Even in a secular society like ours, you and I could generate a list of dozens of such gods: Thor, Zeus, Neptune, Baal, Marduk, Ra, Mars, Juniper, Saturn. Our language is littered with them: Thursday is Thor's day, Wednesday is Woden's day, and so on. If anything, Gervais's number of three thousand is probably on the conservative side.

Humans have believed in thousands, perhaps millions, of gods. The worship of most of them appears to have fallen by the wayside. Because of that, it's possible to believe a story that goes something like this:

> Humans used to believe in lots of gods. They were how we once made sense of the natural world or found comfort in our suffering. In Christopher Hitchens's words, they were our "first and worst" shot at explaining everything. However, most of those gods have been abandoned, victims of their own lack of evidence, or their weak explanatory powers. Numbers are trending down. Jews, Christians, and Muslims have narrowed it down to one. And atheists

go one further and have got it to zero. The story of the gods in the West in three words: Many. One. None.

It's a plausible story. It seems to make sense of what we see.

But its chief drawback is that it's not true.

By which I mean that every claim it entails is demonstrably false. It is false that there has been a linear decline in the number of gods humans believe in. It is false to assume that belief in gods functions mostly as a pre-scientific attempt to explain phenomena. And it is false that the atheist worldview is simply the theistic worldview minus belief in God. But the most misleading part of the story is the conflation of two distinct concepts: 'God' and 'the gods'.

The Bible says that "the God who made the world and everything in it is the Lord of heaven and earth and does not live in temples... in him we live and move and have our being" (Acts 17:24, 28).

'God' with a capital G isn't an item on the list of 'things that exist'. He is the ground and source of all existence. And that's a completely different sort of thing.

Hamlet and Shakespeare

Consider the play *Hamlet*. In any printed edition, you'll find a list of the cast: Claudius, Hamlet, Polonius, Horatio, Gertrude, Ophelia, and all the rest. These are the characters who populate the play, the *dramatis personae* of *Hamlet*. The list is the result of an empirical exercise. To write it, you simply need to trawl through the play and make a note of each character as you find them. A faulty list—one that, say, forgot to include Rosencrantz, or mistakenly included a character called Bevan—could easily be fixed in a revised edition. A demonstration of Rosencrantz's presence or Bevan's absence from the play would conclusively settle the matter.

But here's a different question: Is Shakespeare in *Hamlet*?

What if we were to answer that question by the same method we used to establish the presence of Rosencrantz and the absence of Bevan? Such an approach would reveal there to be no Shakespeare. It would conclude that, after an exhaustive search, *Hamlet* was a Shakespeare-free universe.

The problem is one of categories. Shakespeare's existence is of a different order to that of the *dramatis personae*. He is not in the play at all. Rather, he is the one through whom the whole play exists. It is through him that every character lives and moves and has their being.

This is precisely the category error Gervais made in his interview with Colbert. He understood belief in God to be the same thing as belief in 'the gods' and, therefore, the question could be answered in principle with the same method.

Now, granted, the universe is a much larger place than *Hamlet*. Proving a positive is always easier than proving a negative. It's easier to prove where my car keys are (here in my pocket) than to prove, definitively, where they are not (somewhere in this house). The latter requires exhaustive knowledge, which is why most atheists will freely confess they have not definitively proved God's absence from the universe, only that no evidence has been offered for his existence so far.

But the very question is completely wrong. The existence of 'the gods' could be approached in that way. But 'God' is not a thing to be found in our universe. He is the ground and source of all being. Less like a new character in the Marvel universe; more like the director of the franchise. Less like Rosencrantz; more like Shakespeare.

The reasons for God

Nothing I have said so far is an argument for belief in God. It is just a clarification of what the word 'God' means. But understanding the word is crucial for proceeding on the right basis. It helps us to choose the right tools for the task—the task of approaching the God question.[e]

If we are talking about the one who is the ground and source of all being, rather than another being, how might we approach the question of whether such a one exists? I can think of three options: experience, revelation, and reason.

1. Experience: It could be that through prayer, or a vision, or worship, or ecstasy, or beauty that one could encounter God. There might be some way, in other words, of encountering God directly. We could reach out to him.
2. Revelation: It could be that God decided to reveal himself—just as Shakespeare could, if he so chose, reveal information about himself in his play. He could even make himself a character within it. He could write himself into the play. He could reach out to us.

e If you want to take a deep dive into this topic, you could read DB Hart, *The Experience of God: Being, Consciousness, Bliss*, Yale University Press, 2014.

3. Reason: It might be possible to infer or deduce the existence (or probable existence) of God. There might be arguments that establish God's existence. Or it might at least be possible to show that his existence is likely. We could think it out.

Most of the rest of this book rests on the conviction that God has indeed revealed himself (option 2). We believe he has both revealed information about himself and, more than that, written himself into the play. And this book is written in the hope that the story of God's revelation will lead you towards an experience of God (option 1), an experience the Bible describes as repentance and faith.

Given that the rest of the book is about revelation and experience, let's say something here about reason (option 3).

Reason and God

Can reason prove the existence of God? Some say yes. The philosopher Alvin Plantinga says there are two- to three-dozen very good arguments for God's existence—arguments that are valid in their form and compelling in their force.

We'd like to put forward a more modest claim: that belief in God is reasonable. Here are three arguments we find suggestive, if not compelling.

1. There is something rather than nothing

There is something rather than nothing. The question is, "Why?" And the answer of classical theism is, "God".

A number of objections spring to mind.

First, someone may ask, "But who caused God?"

This objection misunderstands the meaning of the word 'God'. God is by definition the uncaused cause, the uncreated creator, the play's author. To ask the question "Who made God?" is a little like someone, on hearing that Shakespeare wrote *Hamlet*, dismissing the answer by saying, "Ah, but who wrote Shakespeare?" No-one wrote Shakespeare. Shakespeare is not that sort of thing. To ask "Who made God?" is to ask an internally contradictory question. It is to ask, "Who made the unmade?" The question is answered in the asking.

Second, others have objected with, "Why does the universe need a cause? Can't it just be eternal?"

On a slightly technical point, the argument itself doesn't rely on there being a moment of creation. Aristotle, for example, believed the universe was eternal and believed in the necessary existence of God. The argument hinges on the concept of contingency rather than creation. Aristotle didn't believe the universe was created, but simply that it was contingent. That is, it must rely on something else for its existence.

But it so happens that, through Hubble's discovery of an expanding universe, a significant scientific consensus has emerged. The universe is not eternal. To the best of our knowledge, there was a beginning, a Big Bang. It was not, and then it was. Reason wants to know who or what caused that. To refuse to even pose the question "What caused the universe?" is to abandon reasoning altogether.

Lawrence Krauss has mounted a gallant argument that we live in a universe in which something could indeed come from nothing. His book *A Universe from Nothing* is fascinating and mind-blowing. But the philosopher, not to mention the average reader, may get the impression that Krauss's definition of 'nothing' is somewhat, well, eccentric. He describes 'nothing' as "empty space", "equal amounts of matter and antimatter", and "space filled with constant energy density".[3] Krauss's version of 'nothing' sounds to philosophers suspiciously like what the rest of us call 'something'. The moment you start applying adjectives to 'nothing', telling us what it's like and explaining some of its more interesting properties, I think we can all safely conclude you're not talking about 'nothing'.

2. Reason itself points to God

Humans are able to reason. Why is that? Philosophical naturalism says that reason is simply an adaptive advantage. The process of evolution selects for survival, not truth. Reason exists to the extent that it helps us to eat, hide, run, mate, and fight. 'Mind' is just another word for what brains do. And what brains do is fight for survival, not search for truth.

Why then do we trust what brains do? Why trust those chemical interactions at all?

A few years ago, I (Rory) had the privilege of debating the formerly mentioned Lawrence Krauss in Perth, Western Australia. Our topic was whether or not it is reasonable to believe in God.

I lost. My mum was the only person who thought otherwise.[f] Krauss had better arguments on the night.

---

f   Mum has described my victory to various dinner guests as stunning, emphatic, and overwhelming. As Lou Reed once said, you can't always trust your mother.

His reasoning was better than mine, his arguments more compelling. That was the judgement of those who were following the argument in the room.

But imagine that night, in the room upstairs, that there is a group of scientists watching a scan of our brain activity. They have no access to the audio; they are just watching what is happening in our heads. If someone were to go upstairs and ask those scientists who won, they would reply, "We can't tell you".

Chemical reactions aren't right or wrong, true or false. "Which chemicals reacted more reasonably?" Neither. They're not reasoning; they're just reacting. In this world, no-one won the debate. Winning a debate is meaningless. Chemicals doing stuff in one head sparking chemical reactions in other heads. That's all.

The naturalistic account of the mind is self-defeating. It does not give us good reasons to trust reason itself. But if there is a Mind behind the universe, if there is one who is Reason itself, who has given us the capacity to reason, then we have good grounds for trusting reason.

3. Morality points to God

One of the challenges for Christianity is the problem of evil. One of the challenges for atheism, however, is the problem of 'good'.

Without God, how do we decide something is 'good'? Why not just call it 'people doing stuff'? As the philosopher Alasdair MacIntyre has argued, 'good' in modern Western thought struggles to mean much more than 'I emote positively towards this'. When we say something is 'good', we are saying "Hooray for this!" Our moral instructions to each other become coercive and arbitrary. "I say 'Hooray for this'; you also should say 'Hooray for this'. Why aren't you saying 'Hooray for this'? I am emoting positively towards this thing, so you should too. If you don't, you're a bad person." But why?

Apart from God, things might be pleasant or painful, strong or weak, black or white, high or low, shiny or plain. But it's hard to see on what basis they could be 'good' or 'evil'. How are we making these judgements? 'Good' by whose criteria? These concepts ultimately need something from outside to give them real moral meaning. I hasten to add, this is not to say that you cannot *do* good without God. There are, of course, atheists and agnostics who do great good in the world. You might not need God to do good; our argument is that you do need God to account for the fact that we can call it objectively 'good' and both know what we mean by that word.

Conclusion

These are some of the reasons we think belief in God is reasonable. But, in the end, arguments about God only get you so far. They are, as biblical scholar NT Wright has put it, like "pointing a flashlight toward the sky to see if the sun is shining".[4] In the next chapter, we turn to consider the specific claims Christianity makes about God. Christianity goes beyond the bare claim that God exists. It dares to say that we can know what he's like. We can, in other words, not just know about God, but know God.

3

The Father Almighty, creator of heaven and earth

God and Israel

To simply say "I believe in God" is to declare belief in the God of the philosophers, the God of Aristotle, Maimonides, and Kant. It gets you into the ballpark of theism; it doesn't on its own make you a Christian. Aristotle was a Greek philosopher, Maimonides was a Jewish Rabbi, and Kant was, well, a Kantian. But to say "I believe in God, the Father Almighty" is to be much more specific. It is to declare belief in the God of Israel, the God who is known not just by reason, but through the specific story of his dealings with a specific people. As theologian Robert Jenson once put it, "God is whoever raised Jesus from the dead, having before raised Israel from Egypt".[5]

Christians sometimes criticize the Apostles' Creed for skipping over roughly three quarters of the Bible, the Old Testament. There, we read the story of the nation of Israel. God calls a man named Abraham, and through his children begins a project of bringing blessing and salvation to a world gone wrong. It's a long, gripping tale of miraculous escapes from slavery, wars, tragedies, victories, nation building, national disasters, and renewed hopes.

But the creed seems to jump from God straight to Jesus: "I believe in God, the Father Almighty, creator of heaven and earth. I believe in Jesus Christ..." What happened to, oh, you know, most of the Bible?

The criticism might be fair, but not entirely. Later, we will consider the claim that Jesus was "born of the virgin Mary", which embeds Jesus in the story of Israel. The very title "Christ" is an Old Testament title, presenting Jesus as the fulfilment of that story. Indeed, the whole shape of the creed, the story it tells—from creation to judgement and the world to come—is built on a foundation that comes from the Old Testament.

And even here, as the creed begins, God is called "Father". While the main reference is to God being the Father of Jesus (see the next chapter), there are echoes in the Old Testament of God as a father. In the garden of Eden, Adam is, in one sense, the son of God. Remember, prior to the Industrial Revolution, most of humanity was involved in agriculture, and in that context the relationship between fathers and sons was less domestic and more like a trainee-apprentice relationship. Fathers taught their sons what to do; sons did what their fathers did. That's Adam in the garden: God, Adam's father, brings order to the world; Adam, his son, brings order to the garden.

The father-son relationship extends to the nation of Israel. Several times over, the Old Testament pictures God as Israel's father, and Israel as God's son.[g] Sometimes, this speaks of the special concern and love God has for

g   See, for example, Exodus 4:22, Deuteronomy 32:6, or Hosea 11:1.

Israel (Hosea 11:1). At other points, 'father' is almost a synonym for 'creator'. So in Deuteronomy, Moses sings a song in which he says of God to Israel: "Is he not your Father, your Creator, who made you and formed you?" (Deuteronomy 32:6). Other times, like with Adam, the idea of God as a father puts obligations on Israel to be like their father in the world. Israel is not just God's son, but his "firstborn" son, the exemplary son, setting the tone for the rest of the siblings, bringing credit or shame on their father by their behaviour in the world.

And within Israel, God is particularly the father to the king of Israel. God promises to be the king's father, and the king receives the title of the "son" of God (2 Samuel 7:14). This, you might guess, is important background to what we mean when we talk about Jesus as the "Son of God".

The doctrine of the Trinity

God became the father of Israel. But the creed is hinting at something more. I (Rory) became a father in the year 2005. God, according to the creed, was a father prior to having created anything. Father of what? Or, more accurately, father of whom?

The answer of the Christian faith is that, before God was the creator of the world, he was already the Father of the Son. God was not always creator, but he was always Father. He always had a Son. And this Father and this Son loved each other before the creation of anything at all, bound together by the presence of the Spirit. Love, in other words, is older than creation. There was a time when you were not, when I was not, when the world was not, but there was never a time when love was not. God has always loved his Son. The creation of the world was not because God cried out in eternity, in the words of Freddie Mercury, "Can anybody find me somebody to love?" He already had someone to love. God created the world not to fill a lack, but from the overflow of a love already there.

The creed (and, consequently, this book) is shaped around the idea of God as Father, Son, and Spirit. This is the distinctly Christian claim that God is one being in three persons. How many gods are there? One. How many persons are there in God? Three. It's a bit weird. It stretches human language to its breaking point. And it's one of the best things about the Christian faith.

What do we mean by the Trinity? Let's try and capture it in three moves.

First, there is only one God. Not two, three, seven, or ninety-four. Only one God.

Second, that one God exists in three persons: Father, Son, and Holy Spirit. One God, three persons.

Third, each of those three persons is fully God, not a part of God. They do not each have a 33.33% share of the deity and, when put together, equal God. No, when you encounter the Father, the Son, or the Spirit, you encounter God in full, not God in part.

The doctrine of the Trinity is simple and precise. But the reality to which it points—the nature of God—is mysterious and beyond our grasp. All analogies fall short of the reality to which they point. There is nothing else in the world that is like the Trinity: not water as steam, ice, and liquid; not a clover with three leaves; not a person as parent, child, and sibling. In each case, the analogies hinder more than they help. Better to just say: "God is like this, and nothing else in all creation is".

But that's okay, isn't it? I mean, if we are talking about the God who is there, there's every reason to expect that he'll be beyond our grasp and above our understanding. The doctrine of the Trinity is our guardrail against idolatry. It directs us to worship and adore the God who is there, not the god we imagined was there. Who would make this up?

The doctrine of the Trinity is hard to grasp in the abstract, but it is essential to make sense of the Christian story. With it, your head can start to explode. But without it, everything else in the Christian life blows up. The nature of our salvation, the forgiveness of sins, the nature of prayer, the hope of life with God—all falls apart if God is not Father, Son, and Spirit.

Copernicus (1473-1543) is popularly credited with establishing that the sun, and not the earth, is at the centre of our solar system. To believe this is quite a feat of imagination. Everything in our senses suggests the earth is really the centre. How do we know the earth in fact revolves around the sun? Why do we believe this? No-one got into a rocket, measured the diameter of the solar system and then located the sun in the middle. Rather, we have been shown two things. First, we have seen how messy the movement of the planets is when you put the earth at the centre. Second, when you put the sun at the centre, suddenly the movement of all the planets makes sense.

The doctrine of the Trinity is like that. It's not a doctrine that makes sense in itself, so much as the doctrine without which nothing else in the Christian life makes sense. It sits at the centre of our faith, like the sun at the centre of our solar system, the X that makes sense of the Y, the unique centre around which all our worship, prayers, service, and life orbit. And it leads us not to perfect understanding, but to adoration.

The creator God, us, and the creation

The belief that God is the creator of heaven and earth orients us to the world in a certain way. A purely secular view of things might suggest the world is a raw fact: something that simply is. An atheist might have feelings of gratitude for the wonders of the universe, but those feelings are some sort of misfiring of prehistoric instincts, the residue of an ancient habit of ascribing will and personhood to impersonal forces. There is, the atheist now knows, no-one to thank.

Many spiritual views spin the physical world negatively. Either it's a distraction from the 'real business' of life, which is spiritual, or it's a positive evil: the product of a lesser god with malevolent intentions towards us.

Over and against all these views, the Christian view invites us to see the world not as raw fact, or threat, or evil, but as a good gift. The Christian faith is an invitation to delight in the concrete realities of a world which God made, and which God made *good*. It is an invitation to give thanks to some *one* for every *thing*. All of it. The fierce sun beating down on the desert sands, the white of the waves as they smash against the rocks, the root systems of trees, the smell of peat. Music, books, and lovemaking; whiskey, potatoes, and butter. The sound of a cricket ball when it finds the centre of the bat and is smashed for a six, the laughter of children, the smell of sautéing onions, the architecture of Gaudi, the 'whomp' of a door closing on a European car, the sky at dusk. Old men getting the giggles, children playing chasey, one of Bach's cello suites, the scent of woodfires, the feel of water. All of these are invitations to praise, incitements to worship. They are an opportunity to give thanks to the God who made them.

And these are not gifts once given, now forgotten. According to the Bible, God not only made the world but sustains it. He not only gave it once, but continues to give it again every day, holding it up by his word of power. Science is based on the assumption of predictability, the working hypothesis that the world is not random, but ordered. This is true, and science proceeds on this basis. But the world is not predictable in the way a watchmaker's watch is predictable: continuing to do what the watchmaker intended, even in the watchmaker's absence. Rather, the world continues to do what it does because God continues to make it happen. It is predictable, and science can proceed, because God keeps saying to the processes of creation, "Do it again!" As GK Chesterton puts it:

> Because children have abounding vitality, because they are in spirit fierce and free, therefore they want things repeated and unchanged. They always say, "Do it again"; and the grown-up person does it again until he is nearly dead. For grown-up people are not

strong enough to exult in monotony. But perhaps God is strong enough to exult in monotony. It is possible that God says every morning, "Do it again" to the sun; and every evening, "Do it again" to the moon. It may not be automatic necessity that makes all daisies alike; it may be that God makes every daisy separately, but has never got tired of making them. It may be that He has the eternal appetite of infancy; for we have sinned and grown old, and our Father is younger than we.[6]

The image-bearers of God

Jesus was once asked (randomly enough) for his policy on taxes. Should we (the 'we' in this case being the Jewish nation, then under the dominion of Rome) pay taxes to our colonial overlords? Should we, in effect, fund our own oppression, and increase the revenue base of a pagan empire?

In response, Jesus asked the crowd for a coin. Holding it up, he asked, "Whose image is this?" The image was, of course, Caesar's. "So give back to Caesar what is Caesar's, and to God what is God's" was Jesus' reply (Matthew 22:21).

We bear not Caesar's image, but God's. Like coins with a picture of the monarch on one side, we are supposed to be embodied pictures of the Monarch of heaven here on earth.[h] We are uniquely stamped with the image of the

---

h   American readers: you will not, of course, have pictures of the queen or king of England on your currency, due to your revolution. It's never too late to come back. No hard feelings.

One who has authority around here. We are God's argument for the existence of God. The rest of the creation is supposed to look at us and at the way we manage our affairs and say, "There is a God, and he is like them". It is our vocation to be the part of the creation that reminds the rest that God is good, and he rules all things well.

Jesus' comment about the coin, then, is not just a comment about what we are. It is, at heart, a comment about whose we are. The coin, bearing Caesar's image, belongs to Caesar. But according to Jesus, if we bear God's image, we belong to God. God's image on us is also his claim on us.

Why don't people believe?

Why, then, don't people believe? If belief in God is reasonable, and if God has gone to the trouble of revealing himself, why don't more people believe? Why doesn't God make his existence plainer?

We humans, it turns out, have a dog in this fight, a conflict of interest when it comes to God. The way the Bible puts this is that we suppress the knowledge of God:

> For since the creation of the world God's invisible qualities—his eternal power and divine nature—have been clearly seen, being understood from what has been made, so that people are without excuse.
>
> For although they knew God, they neither glorified him as God nor gave thanks to him, but their thinking became futile and their foolish hearts were darkened. (Romans 1:20-21)

Here's where it all gets a bit three-dimensional. Knowledge of God necessarily involves knowing ourselves. And this self-knowledge involves the knowledge that we have rebelled against God and, as a consequence, it suits our purposes to ignore his existence. But, like trying to suppress a beachball under the surface of the water, the knowledge of God keeps surfacing. It surfaces in the distorted form of idolatry—worshipping things that are not God.

The Endless Summer was a seminal surf film of the 1960s. It follows the adventures of two surfers from California as they follow summer across the globe, seeking out and surfing some of the most magnificent breaks in the world. Their journey takes them through deserts and across valleys, past mountains and into forests. The whole thing is distilled 1960s gorgeousness, filmed in what looks like an Instagram filter set to 'Wanderlust'. It's beautiful. You should watch it.

Films have credits. What are credits? Credits reflect our moral obligation to acknowledge what came to us by the hand of another. Films don't make themselves. They are the product of vast outlays of human labour, and credit is due to those who worked on them. The credits are a discharging of this duty. They give thanks to the director, the producer, the camera operators, the sound people, and the logistics people. Credits give credit where credit is due.

In *The Endless Summer*, this convention is followed. But throughout the film, they surfed waves they did not make, climbed mountains they did not build, swam rivers they did not form. They had no part in making the best parts of the film, the ocean and its waves. I think they knew it. At the end of the film, we read these words: "We thank Neptune, god of the sea, for the waves."

There it is. Deep down, buried in the credits, and in the deep end of human hearts, is the suppressed knowledge of God finding its way to the surface. We know we didn't create this. We know, somewhere deep down, that life is a gift. A sunset fills us with thankful awe. Food and drink and friendship and love are things we receive rather than create. And every so often, in moments of joy, or guilt, or sorrow, or praise, we find ourselves reaching out for someone somewhere to whom we can give our thanks and praise. Someone to whom we can say sorry, or with whom we can plead for justice, or mercy.

But this instinct surfaces in strange and broken ways—in the form of idolatry, in worshipping created things rather than the creator. We want to thank someone (which is good), and so we make up a sea-god and thank him (which is sad). "Because of these things," says the Bible, "the wrath of God is coming" (Colossians 3:6).

Which brings us to part 2: the person and the mission of Jesus.

Part 2: Jesus

I believe in Jesus Christ, his only Son, our Lord,
who was conceived by the Holy Spirit
and born of the virgin Mary.
He suffered under Pontius Pilate,
was crucified, died, and was buried;
he descended into hell.
On the third day he rose again from the dead.
He ascended into heaven
and is seated at the right hand of God the
Father Almighty.
From there he will come to judge the living and
the dead.

4

Born of the virgin Mary

Two particular Christmases from my (Peter's) child-hood stand out as periods of sheer terror. The first was when my mum found me in the room where she had hidden all my Christmas presents; the second was when I had to play Joseph in the primary school nativity play—my first and last acting role.

More typically, my childhood Christmases in Northern Ireland were (despite the normal family tensions) times of joy. Christmas remains a popular intrusion of the Christian calendar into our increasingly secular culture. And the birth of Jesus and the figure of Mary are delightful, if curious, intrusions into the Apostles' Creed. Let me explain.

Jesus' birth commands a full two lines in the creed. Compare this with his life and teaching (zero), his miracles (also zero), and his exorcisms (another zero). This is curious.

When we turn to the New Testament itself, the puzzle is compounded. Of the four biographies of Jesus ('Gospels'), only two record the birth of Jesus *at all*. Think about that. A full fifty percent of the New Testament Gospel writers decided they could tell you the good news of Jesus without you needing to know anything about his birth. And, apart from a couple of oblique references in the letters of Paul and the book of Revelation, everyone else seems to be able to get along preaching the gospel without mentioning the birth of Jesus. And yet, here it is in the creed, and in our calendar. Why?

The virgin birth of Jesus

Jesus, the creed says, was born of a woman called Mary, who was a virgin. What might this mean? Some have assumed the virginity of Mary is an elaborate effort to avoid an awkwardness about sex. Jesus was holy; sex (it is thought) is inherently a less-than-holy enterprise. If God were to show up in human form on this planet, best to keep sex out of the picture. The problem here is that's simply not how the Bible views sex. Like, at all. Sex is part of God's good creation, a feature of his original design, and a metaphor for divine love. This is a false lead.

Others have thought it to be an explanation of how Jesus could be both God and human. Jesus *was* both God and human (see chapter 5 below), and he was born of the virgin Mary. But the Bible never offers B as an explanation of how A is possible. Jesus isn't a God-man by virtue of having God as his father and Mary as his mother.

More recently, sceptics have suggested that the virgin birth of Jesus is a piece of Greek-style mythology, snuck into the New Testament to give the ever-so-subtle suggestion that Jesus is like one of those figures from the pagan stories who were the offspring of a divine-human sexual liaison.

But again, this is a false lead. Those stories have very little in common with what we find in the New Testament. No-one in those stories of divine-human encounters gives birth, by definition, *as a virgin*. All of them happen in the pre-history of mythology. All of them are consequences of the frequent (and often sexually charged) visits of the Greek pantheon to earth. Jesus, on the other hand, is born to a virgin. His birth is not in pre-history, but under the reign of Caesar Augustus, into a Jewish culture that thought the god-human birth stories of paganism were faintly ridiculous and one of the many things that reminded them how much better it was to worship the one true God, maker of heaven and earth.

One more possibility: given the minor place of the virgin birth in the New Testament, perhaps we should entertain the idea that one of the Gospel writers slightly embellished his account. Perhaps, in the freedom afforded by a lack of sources and unconstrained by modern historiographical conventions, one of the writers saw an opportunity to spice things up a little at the front end of the story.

And yet, despite its low profile in the New Testament, from a historical-sources point of view, the evidence for the strange birth of Jesus is strangely good. Granted, there is nothing like the large body of documentary evidence that we have for the resurrection of Jesus (more on this later). But what we have is, in its own way, remarkable.

There are two main accounts in the New Testament: Matthew and Luke. And, what's more, both Matthew and Luke are completely independent of each other at this point. Matthew didn't copy from Luke; Luke didn't copy from Matthew. Because both writers tell their stories of Jesus' birth so differently, we can be sure that, wherever they are getting their information from, it's not from the same source, nor is it from each other.

And then, throughout the rest of the New Testament, you have a bunch of these little clues that *something* went down around Jesus' birth. In Mark's Gospel, for example, Jesus is referred to as Mary's, but not Joseph's, son. In John's Gospel, the Jerusalem leadership taunts Jesus with the question "Where is your father?"[i] It's all very curious.

Beyond the New Testament, there are non-Christian sources that point to some sort of ambiguity or irregularity in the birth of Jesus. The Greek philosopher Celsus, for example, records a tradition that Mary conceived Jesus through adultery with a Roman solider and gave birth to Jesus outside of wedlock.

Put that all together: two direct accounts of the virgin birth in the New Testament, each independent of each other and drawing on older and independent sources; casual clues and hints at the irregularity of the birth of Jesus elsewhere in the New Testament; and a smattering of alternative takes on the birth of Jesus in the non-Christian literature. By the canons of ancient history, that's an impressive little cache of material. It doesn't *prove* anything, of course. At least, it doesn't prove that Jesus was born of a virgin. But it's precisely the kind of literary smoke that streams up from some sort of historical fire. There was something strange about Jesus' birth. Matthew and Luke weren't generating literary flourish. They were offering their explanation of the puzzle. It was strange, they think, because Mary was a virgin.

---

i   See John 8:19. Note also in the same chapter, Jesus' interlocutors say, "We are not illegitimate children", with the possible implication that Jesus is (John 8:41).

Three truths of the virgin birth

Positively, then, what does the virgin birth mean? Three things.

1. It's a sign

According especially to the Gospel of Matthew, the virgin birth is a sign. Matthew quotes from the Old Testament prophet Isaiah in which, hundreds of years before Jesus, the prophet says a young woman would be with child, and the birth of that child would be a sign that God was about to act decisively (Isaiah 7:14). That passage is partially fulfilled within the book of Isaiah itself, but Matthew picks it up and says: It's happening again! Isaiah's prophecy is being perfectly fulfilled! God is about to act, and the virgin birth is a sign of God's coming action.

2. A new creation

In the Gospel of Luke, the virgin birth is also a sign of God's new work in the world. Luke records the angel saying to Mary, "The Holy Spirit will come on you, and the power of the Most High will overshadow you" (Luke 1:35).

In the original creation story, the Holy Spirit is said to have "hovered over" the waters of the deep, as if midwife to the creation of the world. And so too here, the Spirit hovers over Mary's womb as God begins his work of new creation in and through Jesus.

3. The story of Israel

Finally, I think in both Luke and Matthew, as well as in the creed itself, the virgin birth connects Jesus with the story of Israel through the figure of Mary.

Virgin births are not a regular trope in the Bible. Indeed, the only virgin birth in the whole Bible is Jesus'. But throughout the Old Testament, the people whom God raises up to rescue his people are often marked out by strange births: Abraham and Sarah have Isaac in their very old age; Moses is born and then hidden in the Nile by his mother; barren Hannah gives birth to the prophet Samuel; and so on. God uses strange births to signal significant new chapters in the story of Israel. Jesus' birth embeds him in this same story. He is born of the faithful daughter of Israel, Mary; born under unusual circumstances, as Israel's redeemers so often were. Jesus, says the virgin birth, is part of Israel's story.

The early church (and sadly, not only the early church) sometimes allowed anti-Semitic attitudes to be fostered in its midst. Some people would just prefer it, all things being equal, if Jesus was not Jewish, and if Christianity wasn't tethered to Israel's story. But the phrase "born of the virgin Mary" sits in the creed, refusing to cut Jesus from his Jewish heritage, either biologically or culturally. Jesus, being the son of Mary, is also the son of Israel.

One of us

Jesus entered our world, not through a space-time portal, but through a birth canal. He wept (John 11:35), experienced hunger (Matthew 4:2), grew tired (Luke 8:23), became thirsty (John 4:7), and agonized (Matthew 26:38). He experienced the death of one parent and arranged the care of the other (John 19:27). He ate and drank, slept and woke, needed to be with people, and needed time alone. He was "fully human in every way" (Hebrews 2:17).

Edward Shillito captured this reality in his poem 'Jesus of the Scars', a reflection on the horrors of World War I:

The other gods were strong; but Thou wast weak;
They rode, but Thou didst stumble to a throne;
But to our wounds only God's wounds can speak...[7]

This is the doctrine of the incarnation, the teaching that Jesus, truly God, was in every way truly one of us. His birth to a virgin does not *explain* how this is possible, but it points us towards the mystery.

A doctrine on guard

The virgin birth of Jesus, in and of itself, is not a big deal measured by the airtime it's given in the New Testament. It's almost tempting to move on and bypass it altogether. But the creed forces us to stop here on the way through. I'm glad it does. A bit like a speed bump as we drive into a built-up area, it forces us to slow down and ask what sort of story the Christian story is. And what sort of story is it? It's a rescue story, like those stories in the Old Testament. It's a Jewish story, a part of that nation's history. And it's a story about the Son of God becoming a real-life human. For many in the early church, it would have been easier—metaphysically, aesthetically, and epistemologically—to believe that Jesus seemed like one of us but was not. God appearing as a human? Sure. But God with a mum? God with a people and a language? God with teeth and toe-nails? Ew!

The Swiss theologian Karl Barth puts it in these words:

> The Church knew well what it was doing when it posted this doctrine on guard, as it were, at the door of the mystery of Christmas. It can never be in favour of anyone thinking he can hurry past this guard.[8]

I, for one, am glad the virgin birth has been stationed here, at the door of the mystery of Christmas.

Conclusion

In the final book of CS Lewis's Chronicles of Narnia, *The Last Battle*, the children are caught in the crossfire of a fierce battle. On top of a hill, there is a door to a small shed, which they enter to escape the danger. But they discover the door is the entry point not to a tiny shed, but to a vast world of sweeping grasslands and limitless horizons.

As the characters comment on this extraordinary fact, a shed in which the inside is vastly bigger than the outside, Lucy remarks: "Yes, in our world too, a stable once had something inside it that was bigger than our whole world."

5

Lord, Christ, and Son of God

A good friend of mine (Rory's) studied at Oxford university and, through a choir group, was able to tour the world and meet some very impressive people. Presidents, royalty, and leaders of arts and industry all heard the group and met my friend. This friend, not a consumer of popular culture, once sat down next to a movie director at a formal reception in the USA. His name didn't ring a bell. To make conversation, my friend politely asked, "So, George, what sorts of movies do you make?" George apparently made science fiction films. "Splendid! Might I have seen some of them?"

"Have you seen *Star Wars*?" replied George *Lucas*.

"No", said my friend honestly. "Was it popular?"

I'm sure George Lucas found it all rather refreshing to talk with someone who didn't know who he was. For one small moment, the creator of the most iconic science fiction franchise of all time just got to be 'George'.

Who was Jesus? The question by itself is tautologous. We answer it by asking it. Jesus was Jesus, of course. But when we ask a question like that, we are asking something more. My friend knew that the bloke sitting next to him was called 'George Lucas'. But he didn't really know who that was. He has no idea what that name carried with it. In that same spirit we want to ask, who was Jesus?

The creed's answer is that Jesus is "Christ", "God's only Son" and "our Lord". Let's break that down a bit.

Jesus *Christ*

Jesus (or 'Yeshua' as he would have been known around the village) is a first name. To call Jesus 'Jesus' implies nothing more than that you call people by their names.

To add 'Christ' to the name Jesus is to make the additional claim that Jesus was the fulfilment of Old Testament expectations, the hope of Israel and the world, the longed-for Messiah ('Messiah' simply being the Hebrew version of the Greek word 'Christ'). This is who Jesus was claiming to be when, for example, he rode that donkey into Jerusalem. He was claiming to be the son of David, the legitimate claimant to Israel's throne. It's clearer in English if you reverse the order and talk about Christ Jesus, or insert the definite article, as in "Jesus the Christ". However you do it, it's worth being clear on this point: 'Jesus' is a name; 'Christ' is a title.

Our Lord

What does it mean to affirm that Jesus Christ is "our Lord"? Two things at least.

First, as implied by the word 'our', to say "Jesus Christ our Lord" is to say something about Jesus' relationship to us. He is not the Lord of God his Father, but he is our Lord.

To say that Jesus is 'Lord' is to say that he has authority, that God has appointed him to have power, sovereignty, a legitimate rule, a realm. The striking claim of the New Testament is the extent of this rule. At the end of the first Gospel in the New Testament, the Gospel of Matthew, Jesus says to his followers:

> "All authority in heaven and on earth has been given to me. Therefore go and make disciples of all nations, baptizing them in the name of the Father and of the Son and of the Holy Spirit..." (Matthew 28:18-19)

The amount of authority given to Jesus is total: all authority. The geography of his realm is impressive: heaven and earth. And the source of his authority is unassailable: God. In this way and to this extent, he is Lord.

What is interesting is the action plan that follows. In Jesus' world, parts of the empire were regularly packaged up and handed over to local rulers to do with what they willed. "All authority in Judea and Samaria has been given to Herod" are words you could imagine on the lips of Caesar. Therefore, what? Therefore, go and rule over them—collecting taxes and exploiting resources for yourself (so long as Caesar's interests are maintained).

But here, Jesus is given *all* authority over *all* things for *all* time. What does he do with that? He sends his disciples to go and "make disciples of all nations... teaching them to obey everything I have commanded you" (Matt 28:19-20). Jesus, upon being given authority over the universe, immediately embarks on an education program. Not guns, but gospel; not eradication, but education; not conquests, but compassion; not tax, but teaching. A worldwide empire established by baptism and education.

One day, that time will come to its end, and Jesus will wrap things up in judgement and salvation. But for now, we have the opportunity for a peaceful surrender. We have the opportunity to change sides. To enlist with Jesus, and to come under his instruction, rule, and care. He is the Lord; we are invited to call him our Lord.

In World War II, hostilities in the Pacific ended on 2 September 1945. At that point, the allies had won, the victory was clear, the war was over, and Japan surrendered. But the news of the victory sometimes took months, even years, to get to remote theatres of the Pacific. There are stories of Japanese soldiers who continued to hold out on far-flung islands, either ignorant or unconvinced that the war had ended. In some cases, it took visits from their previous commanding officers to convince them they could stand down from their posts, lay down their weapons, and enter into the new peace.

We are like those soldiers. Jesus has won. He has been appointed Lord and Christ. Yet we continue to behave as if that is not the case. And the gospel message is that Jesus comes in peace to all nations, seeking disciples. To lay down our weapons, abandon our posts, and acknowledge his rule is what it means to say, "Jesus Christ our Lord".

Was Jesus God?

Finally, Jesus is (according to the creed) "God's Son". He is 'Lord' to us, but 'Son' to God. But what does it mean to affirm that Jesus is God's Son?

The New Testament teaches the deity of Jesus Christ. It does so carefully, subtly, but unambiguously. John's Gospel, for example, begins by saying that Jesus "was with God" and "was God" (John 1:1). And at the end of that Gospel, Thomas addresses the risen Jesus as "My Lord and my God!" (20:28). To say Jesus is God's 'Son' is to say that he shares in the divinity of his Father. To see the Son is to have seen the Father. Put more baldly, to see Jesus is to have seen God (14:9).

This logic works the other way around. If Jesus is God, and if to see Jesus is to have seen God, then Jesus' capacity to connect us to God is not just impressive; it is unique. In Jesus' own words:

> "I am the way and the truth and the life. No-one comes to the Father except through me." (John 14:6)

To know Jesus is not just to know about God. It is not simply to have good information about God. It is to know and connect with God himself.

Conclusion

"If only God would show himself—then I would believe." The claim of the New Testament is that this has happened. There was once a group of people who, in the face of a first-century Jewish teacher, saw the face of God.

We do not now see Jesus. But, in another sense, we can see Jesus. Through the pages of Scripture, and by the power of the Holy Spirit, we can see him. We can know the one who was known by those who knew him to be God with us. Or, to flip it the other way, God, it turns out, looks like Jesus. To see him and know him is not to line up behind yet another human teacher who may or may not have had some insights into the deity. It is, rather, to encounter God himself.

Philosopher John Hick taught that all religions are of equal value. He conceded, however, that:

> If Jesus was indeed God incarnate, Christianity is the only religion founded by God in person, and must as such be uniquely superior to all other religions.[9]

The point is well made. As CS Lewis put it, Christianity is either infinitely important or not important at all. The only thing it cannot be is moderately important. Jesus the first-century prophet and healer is the Christ, the Lord, and the Son of God. Which, as they say on the internet, is huge if true.

6

Suffered under Pontius Pilate

Gold for Australia!

For obvious reasons, the Olympic Winter Games have not traditionally been an event at which Australia expects to snatch a lot of gold. Which made the 2002 victory of Australian speed skater Steven Bradbury very surprising and so very sweet.

Bradbury was lucky to even make it to the 1000 metres final, made possible when another competitor was disqualified. On the day of the final, he was settled at the back of the pack, coming a solid last, seemingly resigned to his fate.

And then, 50 metres from the finish line, with Bradbury on track for the wooden spoon, it happened. One skater tripped. Then another. Within seconds, all four skaters in front of him had crashed. And Bradbury, with plenty of time to correct, and with a smile on his face that could power a medium-sized city, sailed past them and took the gold.

Australians can list off the names of a dozen Summer Olympic athletes without blinking: Dawn Fraser, Cathy Freeman, Ian Thorpe, and the like. But we all know only one name of a Winter Olympian: Steven Bradbury.

Pontius Pilate

Which brings us to Pontius Pilate.

Pilate (pronounced as you'd pronounce 'pilot', as opposed to the popular exercise program 'pilates') is today perhaps the best-known figure of the Roman administration from the first century. More than Augustus, or Tiberius, or Caligula, my bet is that the name 'Pilate' registers with more people today than any other Roman name of that time.

But here's the thing: Pontius Pilate was a lightweight. He was an ambitious, mid-tier Roman administrator, sent to the exact place no ambitious man wanted to go: Israel. Israel was a strange place, occupied by a highly religious people whose passions for their God and their traditions were likely to flare up into riots at any moment. No-one wanted that job.

But we know Pilate's name. To put this in perspective, it would be like a time traveller going to the year 4020, walking into a school to teach them about 20th-century history, and discovering that some of the students had heard of Winston Churchill, a few knew of Nelson Mandela, but pretty much everyone knew the name of Ray Thompson, the former mayor of Lithgow.

Apart from Jesus, the creed references two other people by name: Mary and Pilate. Mary is associated with Jesus' birth, Pilate with his death; Mary with his reception, Pilate with his rejection; Mary with his flourishing, Pilate with his suffering. He was born of the virgin Mary; he suffered under Pontius Pilate.

The mention of Pilate is the first indication in the creed that there's anything wrong with the world at all. Apart from Pilate, the story the creed tells bounces along from the creation of the world to the birth of Jesus without so much as a hint that anything is out of place. Perhaps its authors assumed that by reading your Bible or looking out your window, you could establish something was wrong with the world all on your own. At any rate, if there's something wrong with the world, the first part of the creed makes no mention of it.

But then, in comes Pilate—like a dirty dog walking into a nice room, as Karl Barth once put it. And what does Pilate do? Causes Jesus Christ to suffer. Maybe what's wrong with the world could be summarized in the words "he"—he who touched lepers, healed the bleeding woman, declared freedom for the captives, loved his enemies—"he suffered under Pontius Pilate".

In a 2016 episode of the long-running radio show *This American Life*, contributor Jack Hitt tells the following story:

> Well, it all began at Christmas two years ago, when my daughter was four years old. And it was the first time that she had ever asked about what did this holiday mean. And so I explained to her that this was celebrating the birth of Jesus. And she wanted to know more about that. And we went out and bought a kids' Bible and had these readings at night. She loved them, wanted to know everything about Jesus.
>
> So we read a lot about his birth and about his teaching, and she would ask constantly what that phrase was. And I would explain to her that it was "Do unto others as you would have them do unto

you". And we would talk about those old words and what that all meant, you know?

And then one day, we were driving past a big church, and out front was an enormous crucifix. She said, "Who is that?" And I guess I'd never really told that part of the story. So I had this sort of "Yeah, oh, well, that's Jesus. And I forgot to tell you the ending. Yeah, well, he ran afoul of the Roman government." This message that he had was so radical and unnerving to the prevailing authorities of the time that they had to kill him. They came to the conclusion that he would have to die. That message was too troublesome.

It was about a month later after that Christmas. We'd gone through the whole story of what Christmas meant, and it was mid-January. And her preschool celebrates the same holidays as the local schools. So Martin Luther King Day was off. So I knocked off work that day, and I decided we'd play and I'd take her out to lunch. And we were sitting in there, and right on the table where we happened to plop down was the art section of the local newspaper. And there, big as life, was a huge drawing by a 10-year-old kid in the local schools of Martin Luther King.

And she said, "Who's that?" And I said, "Well, as it happens, that's Martin Luther King. And he's why you're not in school today. So we're celebrating his birthday. This is the day we celebrate his life." And she said, "So who was he?" And I said, "Well, he was a preacher". And she looks up at me and goes, "For

Jesus?" And I said, "Yeah. Yeah, actually, he was. But there was another thing that he was really famous for, which is that he had a message."

And you're trying to say this to a four-year-old. This is the first time they ever hear anything, so you're just very careful about how you phrase everything. So I said, "Well, yeah, he was a preacher and he had a message". She said, "What was his message?" And I said, "Well, he said that you should treat everybody the same no matter what they look like".

And she thought about that for a minute. And she said, "Well, that's what Jesus said". And I said, "Yeah, I guess it is. I never thought of it that way, but yeah." And that is sort of like, "Do unto others as you would have them do unto you". And she thought for a minute and looked up at me and said, "Did they kill him too?"[10]

He suffered under Pontius Pilate.

A life of suffering

The creed jumps straight from Jesus' birth to his death. "Born of the virgin Mary, suffered under Pontius Pilate." What happened to his life? What were they playing at?

Maybe it's an omission. But maybe something profound is going on. Maybe the early Christians thought the life of Jesus could be summarized in the words "he suffered".[11]

There's a poem in the Old Testament, in the prophecy

of Isaiah (chapter 53), that the early Christians understood as applying to Jesus. Hundreds of years before Jesus was born, the prophet wrote these words:

> He had no beauty or majesty to attract us to him,
>> nothing in his appearance that we should desire him.
> He was despised and rejected by mankind,
>> a man of suffering, and familiar with pain.
> Like one from whom people hide their faces
>> he was despised, and we held him in low esteem.
> (Isaiah 53:23)

The life of Jesus was very full. It was full of miracles, teaching, healing, exorcisms. He had friends. He went to dinner parties (lots of dinner parties). He travelled. He participated in religious festivals. He argued with religious teachers. He rested, caught boats, broiled fish, started riots, and fell asleep in the stern of a boat.

But there was something about where his life was heading, and how that goal shaped everything he did, that meant Christians could summarize his life in two words: "he suffered".

Conclusion

The creed mentions three people from history: Jesus, Mary, and Pilate.

A first-century Jewish prophet, a Jewish peasant woman, and a mid-tier Roman official. Jesus, the Son of God. Mary, who says yes to God. And Pilate, who says no.

In her play *The Man Born to Be King*, Dorothy L Sayers

imagines Pilate's wife coming to report the content of a dream to her ambitious husband. Pilate asks what the dream was about. She replies:

All I can remember is a great crowd of people... I don't know who they were or where they were. All I remember is that they were speaking in a dozen or more languages. And they were all saying the same thing, over and over and over, "Suffered under Pontius Pilate, Suffered under Pontius Pilate, Suffered under Pontius Pilate".[12]

7

Crucified, died, buried, he descended into hell

The creed says that Jesus was crucified. This alone should be sufficient to establish that he died. Including the details that he "was crucified, died, and was buried" and that he "descended into hell" seems surplus to requirements. If I read in a newspaper that such-and-such a criminal was executed by lethal injection, I can infer the rest. I am not left wondering what happened next.

The creed, by labouring the point, creates a puzzle. Why? Why this emphasis?

It certainly causes us to slow down.

The biblical Gospels are like this. They do the cinematic equivalent of a movie switching from a montage approach to the life of Jesus to a real-time account of his suffering and death. The creed, having raced over his life, lingers at his death. He suffered under Pontius Pilate.

And he was crucified.

And he died as a result of that crucifixion.

Then his dead body was buried.

And then he descended into hell.

From the creation of the world to the birth of Jesus at breakneck speed. And then, at his death, we suddenly go into slow motion. It is as if the creed is saying, "Pay attention! This bit is really important."

Crucified, died, and buried

It is almost impossible for us today to capture the strangeness of mentioning, let alone celebrating, the crucifixion of Jesus.

In the first century, 'crucifixion' was not a metaphor. No-one said, "Oh, man, I got *crucified* at work today". In fact, Roman etiquette books reminded people to never mention crucifixion in polite company.

Crucifixion was cruel and unusual by design. The whole theatre of it—the nakedness, the loss of control of bodily functions, the slowness of the death, the public spectacle as you were thrust up into the view of all—it was all calculated to bring you shame. No Roman citizen could be crucified. It was reserved for non-citizens, for slaves, and for outlaws. The Romans would happily decapitate a citizen who had committed a serious crime, but not crucify them. Come on! We have standards, people!

Those who were crucified bore on themselves the full weight of Rome's military might and judicial power. As their bodies were left to rot or become food for birds, they were a reminder to the rest of what happens to those who challenge Roman order.

For a Jewish person, crucifixion had an additional layer of meaning. In the Old Testament law, anyone who was "hung" on a tree (or a cross) was "under God's curse" (Deuteronomy 21:23). A Jewish person reading their

Scriptures and looking at a body nailed to a cross didn't have to wonder what it might mean. It already meant something. It meant the person was under God's curse.

Crucifixion wasn't an empty vessel, waiting for Christians to fill it with meaning. It already meant something. Loser. Non-person. Cursed by God. These are the essential meanings of crucifixion. In the Christian faith, we are not stepping into a semantic vacuum, trying to argue that the crucifixion of Jesus meant something after all. We are arguing that it means something *else*. But what?

The clue is there in the next part of that poem by Isaiah:

> Surely he took up our pain
>   and bore our suffering,
> yet we considered him punished by God,
>   stricken by him, and afflicted.
> But he was pierced for our transgressions,
>   he was crushed for our iniquities;
> the punishment that brought us peace was on him,
>   and by his wounds we are healed. (Isaiah 53:4-5)

The Christian faith addressed the problem of the meaning of the cross, not by going around it, but by going through it. Cursed? Yes! Punished? Yes! Crushed? Yes! But why? For our pain and suffering. Our transgression. Our iniquity.

The pulsating heart of the Christian faith is right here. God in Christ stands where we should have stood, receives the punishment we should have received, died the death we should have died. He takes our place: the righteous for the unrighteous, to bring us back to God. This is so important that we'll come back to it again in chapter 12.

The burial of Jesus

Some have argued that this emphasis on the burial of Jesus is to convey that he really did die. Perhaps, though it seems a little excessive. Historically, there are few recorded cases of people surviving a crucifixion.[j] The idea that Jesus might have naturally survived his was unlikely to enter anyone's head. And at any rate, the word 'crucified', like our word 'electrocuted', implied success, not a mere attempt.

Part of the point is historical. In the normal course of events, those who were crucified were left to rot on their crosses or were thrown into a common grave. The refusal of a proper burial was a feature of the process—a final denial of dignity, of humanity. But in the case of Jesus, he was—as the Gospels are at pains to point out—buried. This is not what a first-century person would expect to have happened to the crucified. It is, for that reason, worth noting.

But behind this historical concern is a theological point of some significance. Jesus lived a life that started in the way our lives start (a birth) and ended in the way our lives end (a burial). From a womb to a tomb, and everything in between, he lived our sort of life. He took the human train all the way to its final destination, the grave.

Karl Barth, reflecting on this part of the creed, says:

> It stands there so unobtrusively and simply superfluously. But it is not there for nothing. Some day we

---

j   Josephus, a first-century Jewish historian, records a crucifixion survival in which three people were taken down from their crosses: "Two of them died in the physicians' hands; the third survived." See *Josephus: The Life; Against Apion*, trans. H St J Thackeray, Loeb Classical Library no. 186, Harvard University Press, 1926, p. 155.

shall be buried. Some day a company of men will process out to a churchyard and lower a coffin and everyone will go home; but one will not come back, and that will be me.[13]

Burial is the natural end of a human life, the one-way trip we will all make.

It is also God's judgement on sinful humanity. It is the wages of our sin. Jesus, in his burial, died the death of the creature, and the death of sinners. By slowing down at the point of Christ's death, the creed invites us to linger over the mystery of the incarnation. Fully, completely, actually, without having to cross your fingers or squint or look sideways, Jesus, the Son of God, died. As the early church fathers never tired of saying of Jesus, "That which he did not assume, he could not heal". Jesus did not conduct his mission in a hazmat suit. He completely identified with our humanity in order to heal all of our humanity. Humans go to their graves as finite creatures and guilty sinners. Jesus went there too, not as a guilty sinner, but as a saviour.

The descent into hell

Jesus was crucified, died, and buried. He also descended into hell. This is important. But as Inigo Montoya said in *The Princess Bride*, that word might not mean what you think it means.

In the New Testament, there is a word which most closely aligns with what we think of as 'hell'. That word is *Gehenna*. This is the place of final judgement, the place of separation from God. But the word used in the creed is the word that refers to *Sheol*, or *Hades*, which is, more broadly, the place dead people go.

Our map from the opening chapter is going to help us here. Remember that triple-decker universe? Heaven, earth, and under the earth. Hades is the place under the earth. It is the proper home of the dead.

What is Hades like? It is not a good place, such as heaven. Nor it is a purely retributive place, such as hell. It's a kind of listless, shady, ambiguous, and dark abode. In the Old Testament book of Isaiah, the inhabitants of Hades stir at the latest arrival, like bears stirring from winter hibernation, or like slugs discovered under a sheet of iron. They rise, ghost-like, to greet the now-deceased king of Babylon with the words "You also have become weak, as we are. You have become like us" (Isaiah 14:10).

The psalmist, arguing the case that God should save his life, includes among his arguments that no-one proclaims God's name in Hades. "In Sheol who will give you praise?" (Psalm 6:5, ESV). If you allow me to go to Hades, says the psalmist to God, it will be a bad outcome for both of us. Sheol might not be a place of punishment, but neither is it anyone's favoured destination.

This is what the creed is saying. Jesus died, and, as a result of being dead, he went to the place of the dead, to Hades. But he was not abandoned. Death could not hold him, and God raised him from among the dead. He returned from a destination famous for issuing only one-way tickets.

The harrowing of hell

What, if anything, did he do while he was there? Some would say nothing. But I think we can cautiously affirm three things.

First, Jesus brought the blessings of his death to those who had died in faith before him. What happened to those who knew God and would have trusted in Jesus' death, but were unfortunate enough to be born on the wrong side of the BC-AD line? The New Testament's answer seems to be that Jesus went to the departed saints, heard their cry from the pit, and rescued them from their bondage to death (Ephesians 4:8-10). They trusted in the promises of God, and God came through.

Second, Jesus proclaimed his victory over the evil powers. As Peter puts it, "he went and made proclamation to the imprisoned spirits—to those who were disobedient long ago..." (1 Peter 3:19-20). Between Good Friday and Easter Sunday, it seems, Jesus went to the place of the dead to let his enemies know about the regime change. He proclaimed to them that every knee "in heaven and on earth and *under* the earth" shall bow at the name of Jesus, the Lord (Philippians 2:10). Jesus now holds the keys to death and Hades (Revelation 1:17-18).

Third, Jesus has made death a safe and blessed place for all who now die in him. In the Old Testament, death is never good. It is something always to be avoided, even by those who know God. But by the time of the New Testament, a person like the early Christian missionary Paul can declare that to die is "better by far" (Philippians 1:23). The book of Revelation says, "blessed are the dead who die in the Lord from now on" (Revelation 14:13). Why the change? Because he has conquered the place of the dead. Those who die in the Lord from now on will not experience the ghoulish life of the underworld, but the conscious blessing of God, while they await the resurrection of the body. Those who hope in Christ do not glory in death. Christians still grieve at the death of others, and anticipate their own death with natural apprehension. But Jesus has taken away death's sting; he has rendered it a toothless tiger.

On the strength of these convictions about what Jesus did between Good Friday and Easter Sunday, Christian attitudes to the dead radically changed. Think of the tradition in England and elsewhere of churches being surrounded by the gravestones of former parishioners. Going to church surrounded by the blessed dead. Or think of the early Christians who, as Ben Myers recounts:

> ...would assemble for prayer in tombs. They would worship Christ among the bones of the dead. Believers would raise the bodies of martyrs in the air and parade them through the streets like trophies. At funerals they would gaze lovingly on the dead and sing psalms of praise over their bodies. Such behavior shocked their pagan neighbors. According to Roman law, the dead had to be buried miles away from the city so that the living would not be contaminated. But Christians placed the dead right at the center of their public gatherings.[14]

In the interest of public health, I have no desire to revive these particular traditions. But our society has gone to the other extreme. Death is out of sight, unspoken of, a hushed secret, an embarrassing fact. It is medicalized and marginalized. We don't know what to do with it. Those early Christians approached death differently. They did so from a deep conviction that Jesus descended to the dead, and, in doing so, made death a safe place for all who die in him.

8

On the third day he rose again, he ascended into heaven

Facts and values

Remember as a primary school student the first time you saw a teacher at the supermarket or on the train? It kind of threw you. You'd always thought the teachers lived at school. There was probably a dormitory or something in which they were housed and fed. Each day they were let out to teach. And each evening, as we went off to play and to rest, they presumably returned to their dormitory on the school grounds, preparing to teach again. But the idea that your teachers also had families and went to shops and wore tracksuits—it was just a bit weird. Seeing someone out of the context you associate them with is like that. It throws you. School, not the supermarket, is where teachers go.

Western thought over the last several hundred years has developed some very strict rules about where things 'go'. We hold key binaries as axiomatic: public and private, myth and history, science and religion. These distinctions are so fixed in our minds that we often become aware of them only when they are transgressed. I (Rory) remember in Indonesia being taken aback as my taxi driver, whom

I'd known for all of six minutes, cheerfully asked, "So, which religion are you?" For him, religion was an aspect of public life and therefore a question that could be asked of a stranger. My whole social conditioning has taught me that religion is firmly part of private life, and a matter of discussion only for intimate friends. It was like seeing your teacher in the supermarket: what on earth is religion doing here? Popping up in places it has no business being.

Facts and values are another such binary for us. Fact: the earth revolves around the sun. Value: I like kindness. Facts have a natural home in newspapers, classrooms, and workplaces. Values live around dinner tables, in homes, and in friendship networks. Religion, if it fits anywhere, pairs nicely with values.

Westerners inhabit similar spaces. You *can* talk about religion—but it's normally over food, on a weekend, with people you know well. Why? Because religion is in the values category, not the facts category. It has a spot, and it's best for everyone if it stays there.

The resurrection of Jesus

The creed says that Jesus rose again from death on the third day, and that he ascended into heaven. This resurrection of Jesus complicates the system. Christianity is a religion. Religions deal in values, not facts. Therefore, the resurrection of Jesus is a—well, what is it?

Strangely, at least to most Westerners, the claim that Jesus rose from the dead is, for the New Testament Christians, fact *and* value, history and hope, reality and religion, a thing both known and believed. It conveys a fact *and* it carries a meaning. It is, to quote CS Lewis, the "true myth".[15]

Let's go with the 'true' bit first. Is the resurrection of Jesus true? As in, did it happen? On what basis could the resurrection of Jesus be a thing you know to be true? What sort of evidence do we have for it? The answer is historical evidence.

It's worth labouring the point. We do not have scientific evidence. That is to say, the resurrection of Jesus is not something we know by repeated experimentation with dead bodies. But nor is it a private belief. It's not a conclusion you come to in the privacy of your own home, armed with nothing but your own thoughts.

The claim that Jesus rose from the dead is an irreducibly *public* claim. When the Bible writers claim that he rose, they mean that he rose in space and time. In history. An event that happened in our world. Take, for example, the apostle Paul's summary in his letter to the church in Corinth. The message he received and passed on to the Corinthians was that Jesus:

> ...was buried, that he was raised on the third day according to the Scriptures, and that he appeared to Cephas, and then to the Twelve. After that, he appeared to more than five hundred of the brothers and sisters at the same time, most of whom are still living, those some have fallen asleep. Then he appeared to James, then to all the apostles, and last of all he appeared to me also, as to one abnormally born. (1 Corinthians 15:4-8)

Notice the details. A specific day (the third day). Whole names (Cephas, James). We have groups of real people (the Twelve, the five hundred). Notice the detail that most "are still living". Why tell us that? This account was written in the early 50s of the first century. It's not surprising that a majority of those at an event twenty years earlier are still alive. So why mention it? The obvious reason is that you could talk to them about what they saw. For Paul, the resurrection of Jesus is not something that happens in human hearts, religious services, or in mythic prehistory. The resurrection happened about twenty years before Paul wrote this letter, in our world, and a whole bunch of people saw the risen Jesus.

The claim is that Jesus rose in history. And history is substantiated by documents. So, what sort of documents do we have?

The news is good.

Firstly, what we have is early. It's close to the time of the events recorded. The Gospels are tricky to date, but they come into the form we know them between 30 and 60 years after the events they record. And the sources on which those Gospels are based are very close to Jesus indeed—certainly within decades, probably years (some have argued weeks), of the events they record. In the case of the apostle Paul, we are certain that his writings were written between AD 49 and 64, giving us documents written within twenty years of the events they describe.

Secondly, we have multiple authors writing multiple sources. Sometimes in ancient history, one document is the best we can hope for. It's never ideal, but you have to work with what you've got. However, in the case of the resurrection of Jesus, we have evidence across several authors, writing in different genres (Gospel, letter, 'apocalypse', and so on).

Thirdly, much of the evidence for the resurrection of Jesus is *incidental*. By this we mean that Paul (for example) never sat down to write a life of Jesus, nor did he write with one eye on future historians sifting through his material. Paul was writing pastoral letters to wayward churches, not historical sources for future scholars.

And so, on the basis of multiple historical sources, some very close in time to the events they record, we can state the following with confidence: the early Christians were convinced that Jesus of Nazareth, who was crucified on Friday, 3 April, AD 33 and died at about 3pm that afternoon, was restored to life again on Sunday, 5 April, AD 33.[k] He left an empty tomb behind, and appeared to a wide variety of his followers over a 40-day period. On this basis, they came to believe that Jesus Christ, who had died, was now alive again, and alive forevermore.

The creed asserts, rather than argues for, the resurrection of Jesus. It is not the purpose of this book to lay out the case in great detail. You'll even notice in the paragraph above that we are asserting what the early Christians believed, not that what they believed was true (though of course we share their conviction). But we want to establish

---

k   This is the most likely date for Jesus' crucifixion. The other possibility is 7 April, AD 30. For more information, see PW Barnett, *Bethlehem to Patmos: The New Testament Story*, Paternoster, 1989, pp. 68-69; and HK Bond, *The Historical Jesus: A Guide for the Perplexed*, T&T Clark, 2012, pp. 147-150.

at least what sort of claim this is. The early Christians claimed Jesus had risen from the dead, not in their hearts or in their community's best instincts, but in time and space.

There's always the risk that we bring our culture's values to another culture's texts, putting its ideas into our compartments. We have one compartment for religion, values, and faith, and another for science, facts, and knowledge. The Christian faith is not so neat. Its claim that Jesus rose from the dead can be rejected as false or accepted as true. It can't be relegated to a box in which it's only 'religiously true' or 'true for me'. Either it happened or it didn't. If it didn't happen, you can dismiss Christianity altogether and get on with your life. And, as you do so, spare a thought for Peter and me, living under a profound delusion, which is, at best, a faintly embarrassing prospect for grown men; at worst, the root cause of a bunch of really silly and unnecessary life choices for us both. "Jesus rose from the dead" is not a claim in the same category as "I like toast" or "Good stories make me feel better". If, on a trip to Jerusalem, you should happen to discover what are indisputably the remains of Jesus, do call. Our faith would not and should not survive that kind of discovery.

Fact and meaning

When CS Lewis called the Jesus story the "true myth", he meant that it is 'true' in the sense we have just described. It actually happened. But he also saw it as a 'myth' because myths carry meaning. Something might be true but meaningless, such as the fact that I (Rory) accidentally scratched the side of our car last Tuesday. Something might be meaningful but not 'true', such as the Greek myth of Daedalus and Icarus flying too close to the sun and having the wax on their homemade wings melt. The scratch on my car is true, but teaches me nothing (I already knew I was a bad driver). The story of Daedalus and Icarus might teach me something (don't trust technology, don't be too ambitious), but it's not true. The resurrection of Jesus is true (or, at the very least, is claiming to be true). It is also meaningful.

What does it mean? Here are six core implications to get you started.

Firstly, it means that Jesus really is alive. He is someone we can know, not just know about.

Secondly, the resurrection validates the claims that Jesus made about himself. He made extraordinary claims for himself *and* he rose from the dead. The latter surely opens up giving the former due consideration.

Thirdly, the resurrection completes salvation. It proves that his work of salvation on the cross was effective and accepted by God. God did not allow this truly innocent sufferer to stay dead. The payment he made for sin was accepted by God, and we know that because Jesus did not stay dead.

Fourthly, the resurrection points to the future. We will, the Bible says and the resurrection confirms, be raised with him (see chapter 13). He is God's pilot project for the new creation.

Fifthly, it underlines the value of humanity. Christianity is a humanistic religion. It's about a God who loves humans so much that he became one of them in order to save them. Jesus rose as a truly human being. He will remain a truly human being for all of eternity. In the incarnation, divinity came to humanity. In the resurrection, humanity was taken up into divinity.

Finally, the resurrection of Jesus motivates Christians to live the Christian life. We are called to lives of love and service, freed from the desperation of trying to squeeze every last drop out of the one life we have. If there is a world to come, and a resurrection to be a part of, then life now is more than frantically trying to tick items off a bucket list.

The ascension

Jesus, after his resurrection and appearances, ascended into heaven. What's all that about? It sounds (we accept) super weird. Let's tackle it this way.

My first paid job was in a garden centre. I was thirteen. The task, as described, was to "get the weeds out of a pile of soil". I imagined this to involve maybe half a day's work on a mound of soil as high as my chest. On arrival, I discovered that this was a wholesale garden centre and the pile turned out to be the size of a large suburban house. After two straight days under the hot summer sun, with no tools provided, I did the best job my thirteen-year-old body and brain could manage. I vividly remember the recompense: $40 cash and two bottles of Victoria Bitter beer.

There were so many problems with that arrangement. I hardly know where to begin. At what point did the boss think two bottles of VB were an appropriate part of the salary package for a thirteen-year-old boy? How did he come to the figure of $40 for two days of labour? Where were the tools? What occupational health and safety measures were in place? No hard feelings. Character building and all that. But, from a Human Resources point of view, an odd arrangement at so many levels.

Jesus, according to the Bible, has been given a task, a job, a mission. It is one for which he is eminently qualified. And he has been given the tools to get the job done. This is what the creed is talking about when it says that Jesus "ascended into heaven". It means that the right person is in the right place, doing exactly what he is right to do.

The right person is the resurrected Jesus, the Son of God, who suffered, who conquered death, and who now stands as the "first-born", the first of Humanity 2.0. If the resurrection affirms that Jesus lives forever, the ascension affirms that he reigns forever. A human being has been exalted to God's right hand as Lord forever.

What is Jesus doing there? The image of Jesus having "sat down" comes from the ancient kings, who sat on their thrones, having secured peace for their people. Jesus has done everything that needs to be done to secure our peace, and so he now sits. But he is not inactive. We think of 'sitting down' as what you do when the work is done, but ancient rulers sat down in order to do their work. The rabbis sat in order to teach, as did Jesus when he delivered his famous 'Sermon on the Mount' (Matthew 5:1); the kings sat to exercise their rule, and to this day modern judges sit to indicate the court is in session. That's what sitting means here. By sitting at the right hand of the Father, he is ruling the world, directing the church, praying for those who follow him to persevere (Hebrews 7:25). The right person in the right place doing exactly what he is right to do.

The ascension also points to the obvious fact that Jesus is not here. The absence of Jesus directs attention to a fundamental aspect of the Christian faith. It is exactly that—a faith! Faith is not unreasonable. But faith is not the same as sight. Faith is being convinced—rightly, rationally, and firmly convinced—of something you can't see. The eye-witness accounts of the Gospels and the earth-shattering significance of the resurrection are the basis of the conviction that Jesus is who he says he is. But between those eyewitnesses and the day when we too will become eyewitnesses of Jesus, we live now, not by sight, but by faith.

9

He will come again to judge the living and the dead

It was successful for a few years. Gripping even. Then it started to wane. Plot lines become more and more fantastic. New characters are randomly introduced. Others simply disappear. The idea that it's all heading towards a satisfying conclusion begins to fade. Welcome to Season 5 of your once-favourite television series.

Or to life in the 2020s. For many people in the modern Western world, life is beginning to feel like Season 5. The production values are high. The sets are extravagant. The cast looks good. But it feels like the writers have run out of ideas. It's no longer clear where, if anywhere, it's all heading. We are, as someone (I think it was historian Manning Clark) once put it, "bored survivors in the kingdom of nothingness, surfing and boozing on Bondi, waiting for the Barbarians to come". We find ourselves asking, in the words of singer-songwriter Peggy Lee, "Is that all there is?"

The modern West has a surplus of freedom and a deficit of meaning. To use author Mark Sayers' vivid picture, the freedom tank is full to overflowing, but the meaning tank is nearly empty. We've never had so much freedom, so many choices, such rich options. And we've never been less clear on what the purpose of it all is. The possibility that, perhaps, there is no purpose to anything at all has moved from being the radical suggestion of fringe philosophers to the default assumption of a generation.

We're like the fish at the end of *Finding Nemo*. Having escaped the restrictions of the dental surgery's aquarium, we are afloat in Sydney Harbour. "Now what?" Who knows?

Surplus freedom, and a deficit of meaning. Welcome to Season 5 of Life on Planet Earth.

Does history mean anything?

How do we make sense of our lives? What meaning do our actions have? One possibility is nihilism: don't ask the question, because there is no meaning in history, except the meaning you choose to assign.

Most cultures have not been nihilistic. Historically, the dominant view has been some sort of cyclical understanding of history. In various ways, most ancient religions see history moving in a cyclical motion. We weren't, then we were, and one day we shall not be again. There is winter, spring, summer, and autumn. Life, death, life, and repeat. These traditions helped you to make peace with your existence by understanding it as part of a wider cycle, a great wheel of existence ever returning to its starting point. Dare we say it: the Circle of Life.

The Bible is very different. The Jewish people gave the world something that today seems so normal, but in historical context is very unusual. They said that history was going somewhere. That it is progressing. That life and history are not circular, but linear. That it is less like the seasons, and more like a story, moving from a beginning, through the middle, to an ending. Introduction, crisis, hero, resolution. The end will make sense of the whole. Any time you hear someone talk about the arc of the universe bending towards justice, or worry about being on the wrong side of history, don't thank ancient Greece, or the European Enlightenment, or 21st-century progressives. Send a card to your local synagogue. We got that from Israel.

And this is what Christians affirm in their creed when they say that Jesus "will come to judge the living and the dead". This is the secret, we believe, to life's meaning.

Paul among the philosophers

The apostle Paul once explained this view of the world to the philosophers of Athens. Somewhere in the middle of the first century AD, Paul stood where Socrates had once stood, and taught something Socrates had never taught:

> "The God who made the world and everything in it is the Lord of heaven and earth and does not live in temples built by human hands. And he is not served by human hands, as if he needed anything. Rather, he himself gives everyone life and breath and everything else. From one man he made all the nations, that they should inhabit the whole earth; and he marked out their appointed times in history and the boundaries of their lands." (Acts 17:24-26)

First, the world had a beginning. Second, God made humanity, and made us with a purpose. We are God's off-spring (Acts 17:28). We were made to inhabit the earth in multicultural glory as God's image-bearers. And third, things aren't as they ought to be. We have thought of God as caged in temples, as a being that can be represented by gold, silver, or stone. We were wrong.

All these ideas we have explored in earlier chapters. But notice the shape. History is now not a cycle, but a story. It has a beginning (creation), it has protagonists (the humans) who have a mission (inhabit the earth), and it has a crisis (idolatry). This is a story. Everyone else in the ancient world had stories. But the idea that the history of the world itself was a story—that was new.

Who knows how all this was landing for Paul's audience? Athenians liked new ideas, and this certainly qualified as a new idea. But the real 'mic drop' came at the end:

> "For [God] has set a day when he will judge the world with justice by the man he has appointed. He has given proof of this to everyone by raising him from the dead." (Acts 17:31)

A story needs an ending, a climax. And according to Paul, this is it. Martin Luther King was right—the arc of history bends towards justice. And the role of judge has been allocated. It has been given to Jesus. And we know this because God raised him from the dead.

Myths exposed

I (Rory) grew up in a religious family, and a church context in which the second coming of Jesus was fairly prominent. It was also a source of some anxiety. It was with some surprise that I discovered as an adult that the idea of God's coming judgement is a source of celebration and comfort in the Bible. How can this be?

Three things.

First, the coming judgement of God means that, in the phrase of New Testament scholar NT Wright, everything will be "put to rights".[16] In God's judgement, the cry of the widow will be heard, the orphan will be comforted, the oppressed vindicated, the poor lifted up.

Secondly, the task of judgement has fallen to Jesus. He will come to judge the living and the dead—he who touched lepers, healed the sick, raised the dead, loved the unlovely. The fierce and tender prophet, the man who knew our sorrows, the one who suffered—he is the one God has appointed judge. That's good news.

Thirdly, that judgement will be final. We are promised in the Bible a "new heaven and a new earth" (2 Peter 3:13; Revelation 21:1). We are told that death and Satan will be cast into the fire. That no evil will enter the new city of God. That God himself will wipe every tear from every eye, and there will be no more mourning or sorrow. Everything sad will come untrue.

Implications

On the freeway near my house, there are exit ramps with large red signs saying, "Wrong Way, Go Back". They've always struck me as a very direct piece of communication. I guess when you are travelling at 100kms per hour, a sign that said, "We regret to inform you that the present path on which you are travelling is unsuitable due to the fact that buses regularly travel on the same road at 100kms in the opposite direction to which you are now travelling" would be a case of too much, too late.

The sign has always struck me as forthright and abrupt. But never unloving.

In the same spirit, Paul gave the Athenians an actionable. Given that God is coming to judge the world, he told them, "Repent!" That is, turn around. Go in the other direction. Stop worshipping idols. Turn to Jesus. To a humanity running headlong into idolatry, he said, "Wrong Way, Go Back". In an age of climate crisis, these are not unfamiliar ideas. In the climate crisis, we have a future to be warned of. We have a guilty party (ourselves). And we hear a regular and increasingly urgent call to change our ways—that is, a call to repentance—before it's too late.

We feel duty bound to do the same here. If you are not prepared to meet God, turn around. Turn and trust in Jesus. Jesus himself preached this. Forthright and abrupt. But never unloving.

Hope

There's no getting around it. The Christian claim that God will one day judge the world is bracing. The fact that he will judge each and every one of us is personally confronting.

The coming judgement of God is an inconvenient truth. But it is, we believe, also the secret to life's meaning. Consider the alternative: lives in which no final account is offered or required. A world in which the cries of the oppressed and the crimes of the oppressor are both ignored. An arc of history that bends towards oblivion and unaccountability, not justice. Such a view of the world will leave the meaning tank permanently empty. We will be the escaped fish of *Finding Nemo*, floating on a vast sea of freedom, asking, "What now?"

Part 3: The Holy Spirit and his work

I believe in the Holy Spirit,
the holy catholic church,
the communion of saints,
the forgiveness of sins,
the resurrection of the body,
and the life everlasting. Amen.

Having explored the Christian understanding of God (part 1) and of Jesus Christ (part 2), we now come to the final part of our book, and the final part of the creed. Here, the creed directs us to matters such as life in Christian community (the church), the forgiveness of sins (both God's forgiveness of us and our forgiveness of others), and living in hope of the resurrection of our bodies and the final judgement of God. Consider this a 'try before you buy' scenario. Here is an account of what the Christian life is, in fact, like. It is what the New Testament sometimes calls "life in the Spirit". It is for this reason that the final section of the creed, and therefore the final section of this book, begins with person and work of the third member of the Trinity, the Holy Spirit of God.

10

The Holy Spirit

Water, life, and spirit

I (Rory) live in Western Australia, a state more than twice the size of Texas. Much of my home is a vast, other-worldly landscape of paprika-red dirt, rocky outcrops, and endless plains. In such a landscape, fresh water is rare. Where present, it is impossible to miss. Gorges in the north conceal lagoons of fresh water, harbouring a riot of life amid an otherwise arid landscape. Further south, in my home city of Perth, gardeners bent on reproducing English-style gardens battle with naturally water-resistant sand and a hot, rain-less summer of four or more months. Lawns, deep green from the winter rains, turn yellow within weeks, even days. To our east, maps designate vast inland lakes, such as Kati Thanda-Lake Eyre over the border in South Australia. What the maps do not tell you is that these lakes are waterless most of the time. Kati Thanda fills only once every three years. But when it fills, it becomes a 9,500-square-kilometre inland ocean, teeming with bird life and (impossible though it may sound) full of fish.

Where there is water, there is life.

The Holy Spirit is life. Like fresh water in an arid

landscape, wherever he is, life is also. Indeed, the Holy Spirit is often associated in the Bible with water: he is "poured out", and people are "filled with", or "baptized into" the Holy Spirit. England looks like a land permanently and generously irrigated. The seemingly endless rain of England, one needs to remind oneself, is the price you pay for everything being so green. But such a landscape makes it easy to miss the full force of the Bible's water imagery. In biblical lands such as Israel, or in Western Australia, water comes suddenly and voluminously. It brings with it sudden explosions of life where there previously was none.

The Spirit is like that. "Water" and "Spirit" are closely connected in Scripture for this reason. The Spirit is life. When Kati Thanda is full of life, it's because it's full of water. When a human becomes alive to God, it is because of the Spirit—God's Spirit. In the Bible, when we first meet the Spirit, he is brooding over the unformed earth like a hen over her unhatched chicks (Genesis 1:2). And in the creed, we first meet the Spirit in connection with Mary, in whose womb the unformed embryo is slowly taking the shape of a baby boy. Like a midwife, a brooding hen, or a desert lake, where the Spirit is, there is life.

Literal breath or wind

The word 'spirit' in the Old and New Testaments can also mean 'breath' or 'wind'. Often in the Bible the word is used to describe literal breath or literal wind. In the Old Testament story of Noah, after Noah's flood, we're told that God "sent a *wind* over the earth, and the waters receded"

(Genesis 8:1). Similarly in the New Testament, Jesus says "The *wind* blows wherever it pleases. You hear its sound, but you cannot tell where it comes from or where it is going" (John 3:8). Jesus may be using the literal wind as an illustration, or he may be hinting at something more: the Spirit of God goes wherever he wants to go. So far, so good. The word translated "spirit" can also mean 'wind' or 'breath'.

The spirit of living creatures

Breath animates bodies. What's the difference between a living and a dead body? The living body is breathing. In the biblical sense, that body has a 'spirit'. You see this in the account of the creation of the first man, Adam. The Bible says that:

> ...the LORD God formed a man from the dust of the ground and breathed into his nostrils the breath of life, and the man became a living being. (Genesis 2:7)

Adam begins as a kind of corpse, a body without life. But God breathes life—*spirit*—into him, and the man becomes a living being. In one of the later prophetic books of the Bible, the prophecy of Ezekiel, the prophet sees a vision of a valley of dry bones. Those bones come together as skeletons, then flesh appears on the bones, but the bodies lie in the valley as lifeless corpses. Like Adam, it is only when the Spirit or breath of God comes into those bodies that they become living beings.[1]

---

1   You can follow this up in the Bible in the book of Ezekiel, chapter 37.

The spirit of a person or group

The Bible talks about the ability of humans to be present "in spirit" even if they are physically absent. So, for example, when the missionary and New Testament author Paul writes to a church in the city of Colossae, he can say that he is absent from them in body, but present with them "in spirit" (Colossians 2:5). We speak in similar terms. If I can't come to your football game but tell you "I am with you in spirit", I mean something like "I'm cheering you on and I'll be thinking of you, even though I won't be there physically".

Sometimes this moves beyond metaphor to metaphysics. Evil spirits can be summoned, human spirits can be dislocated from bodies, and 'spirit' is as good a way as any of talking about the state in which humans exist between our death and our bodily resurrection. In some of his last words on the cross, Jesus says to God, "into your hands I commit my spirit" (Luke 23:46). On the least metaphysical reading, Jesus could just be saying, "I'm about to breathe my last breath". On the most metaphysical reading, he's saying, "I'm about to hand over to your care the part of me that will survive my physical death". For what it's worth, I vote for the latter.

What are we saying?

To know God the Father, you need to know what a father is. To know God the Son, you need to know what a son is. And to know God the Spirit, you need to know what a spirit is. What is a spirit? A spirit is breath. Breath gives life. Spirit is how we can be present while physically absent. Spirit is that part of a human that is their inner life, their spiritual centre. Easy.

So, what do we mean when we talk of the Spirit of God? The Spirit is God's breath, God's life, God's presence, and (if I can put it like this) God's spiritual centre. That's what we mean by the Holy Spirit of God.

Life in the Spirit, then, is life lived in tune with God's Spirit. In the Christian life, we are invited to "be filled with the Spirit", to "walk by the Spirit", to "pray in the Spirit", and to labour "in the power of the Spirit". God, in other words, not only commands us to live in a certain way; he also supplies the means by which we can do it. Here are four truths to help us get oriented to life in the Spirit.

1. The Holy Spirit is God's presence

The Holy Spirit is a who, not a what; a he, not an it; a person, not a force.

The word 'Spirit' on its own might push you towards thinking of an impersonal force. But the New Testament consistently describes the Holy Spirit in personal terms. He speaks, teaches, leads, even prays. He can be grieved, resisted, or ignored. He is personal.

Thus, when we say the Holy Spirit is God's presence, we mean more than that he is God's vibe, memory, or power. When we encounter the Spirit of God, we encounter a person, not a thing.

On the night he was betrayed, Jesus promised that when he ascended into heaven he would send "another counsellor" (John 14:16). This counsellor is the Holy Spirit. Jesus is in heaven at the right hand of God. But God is not absent. He has not left us alone. He is with us by his Spirit.

2. The Holy Spirit is the means of new life

The Spirit is the source of new life. Just as God had to breathe into the lifeless body of Adam at the original creation, so too God has to breathe his Spirit into us to bring us to new life in Christ.

According to the Scriptures, after our rebellion against God, we are now "dead in [our] transgressions and sins" (Ephesians 2:1). Of course, we are alive physically—able to run, jump, eat, and swim. But we are by nature dead to God. On our own, we are as likely to respond to God as a dead body is likely to dance the 'YMCA'. For us to hear the call of God *to us* requires God to do something *in us*. God does something objective for us in the mission of Jesus, but he also does something subjective in us, to cause us to respond to what he has done.

Jesus once explained this very thing to the Jewish leader Nicodemus. He told Nicodemus that to enter the kingdom of God he must be "born again". Nicodemus took Jesus with wooden literalism: "How can someone be born when they are old? Surely they cannot enter a second time into their mother's womb to be born!" (John 3:4). But, of course, Jesus was speaking about the Spirit, bringing spiritual life to a spiritually dead humanity.

3. The Holy Spirit is the agent of our transformation

I (Peter) am a sucker for self-help books. I probably read about one a year with the elusive goal of trying to get fitter, be more efficient, or have a less cluttered life. I even bought something from the shopping channel in the hope that it would change my life. It didn't. But then I probably should have known that the "Tuxedo Painting System" was only ever going to disappoint.[m]

God is doing something in his people more ambitious than anything in any self-help book. He is working to make us holy, to transform our characters, to make us fruitful. And he does this work in us by his Spirit, who is the agent of our transformation. So, in Galatians 5, Paul summarizes the Christian life as "walking by the Spirit". This is the idea of walking in dependence on God—a dependence that the Spirit makes possible. The Christian life simply can't be lived without dependence on God, nurtured by the Spirit and expressed in prayer.

This is good news. In the new life that God calls us to, we aren't left to our own devices. We are given God's Spirit, by whose ministry we begin to bear fruit (Galatians 5:22-23). The Holy Spirit is already going that way. The call on us in the Christian life is to "keep in step with the Spirit" (Galatians 5:25).

4. The Holy Spirit is God's power

God calls us to personal transformation and holiness. He also calls us to work in the world to serve the needs of others and to advance the cause of Christ. The former we can call 'ministry' (the word for 'service') and the latter we can call 'mission'. Both our ministry and our mission are enabled by the Holy Spirit of God.

---

m   This was a system where you filled the tube of the roller with paint, which then flowed out into the roller without having to be reapplied to the tray—thus lessening the chance for splashes and so allowing you to do what you have always wanted to do: paint in a tuxedo. The problem was that you had to refill the tube every two minutes. It was a big disappointment and I don't even own a tuxedo.

You see this dynamic in the story of Pentecost, the day the Spirit was poured out on the church. When Jesus had been raised, but had not yet ascended into heaven, he told his disciples to wait in Jerusalem because there they would be "baptized with the Holy Spirit" (Acts 1:5). Interesting. In terms of mission and ministry, the data was in. Jesus had already been born, lived, died for our sins, and been raised to life again. What else did they need? Just get on with telling others! Well, according to Jesus, they needed power:

> "...you will receive power when the Holy Spirit comes on you; and you will be my witnesses in Jerusalem, and in all Judea and Samaria, and to the ends of the earth." (Acts 1:8)

So they waited in Jerusalem. The Spirit was poured out (see Acts chapter 2) and then the gospel went forth from Jerusalem. Jesus sent them the power he promised, power to do his work in the world. This was the promise of God in the Old Testament:

> "And afterward,
>   I will pour out my Spirit on all people.
> Your sons and daughters will prophesy,
>   your old men will dream dreams,
>   your young men will see visions.
> Even on my servants, both men and women,
>   I will pour out my Spirit in those days."
>   (Joel 2:28-29)

In the Old Testament, the Spirit came on key figures (such as priests or kings), empowered them for their tasks, and then left. But after the death and resurrection of Jesus, the Holy Spirit is given to all God's people, all the time, for all sorts of ministry. The Spirit also distributes gifts to God's people for the work he calls us to do. These gifts are both diverse (we are not all given the same gifts) and unified (they are given for the same purpose of building up the body of Christ, which is the church). In short, when God asks us to do something, he always gives us what we need to do it.

Conclusion

As we write, nations across the world are announcing plans to change, radically and permanently, their energy sources from fossil fuels to renewables, from carbon-producing to carbon-neutral. In the plans, cars will still look like cars, trains like trains, and light globes like light globes. The proposed changes are not so much to the outside, but to the inside. We're not getting rid of cars, trains, or light globes. We're just changing how those things are powered.

This is what God is doing by his Spirit. He is changing us from the inside. Changing not our essential identity as humans, but the power source by which we live out the project of being human. To enter into life in the Spirit is like moving from the old energy economy to the new. It is to plug in to God's energy, God's life, God's power source.

How do you enter into the new life of God's Spirit? By asking. God's Spirit is still *God's* Spirit. The Spirit is not something available for purchase on Amazon or exchangeable for goods and services, nor is it discoverable on a local

Buy-Nothing group. There's no second-hand market for God's Spirit. The Spirit is still God's. His to hold onto, and his to give.

But you can ask God. You can ask God to fill you with his energy, to pour out his presence on you, to fill you with his Spirit. You might as well. What's the worst that could happen? Nothing. In which case, the whole episode can be our little secret. But if there is a God, and he has a Spirit, and he has promised to give that Spirit to those who ask him (Luke 11:13), then what do you have to lose? Ask God to make his presence and power known to you by his Spirit. Go on. We dare you.

11

One church

As we saw in chapter 9, in the modern West we struggle to generate meaning. As a consequence, life is often listless, aimless, and disappointing. At the risk of being Captain Obvious, we also struggle to generate community. As a consequence, life is often disconnected, distant, and lonely.

We need community.

But here's the catch: community requires commitment. It requires a decision to forsake a vast range of possible relationships in order to be committed to this set of relationships in particular. And that's the very thing we struggle to do. Like the monkey holding the banana in the cage, we refuse to let go of the very thing we need to let go of, which is our freedom. And we end up never having the very thing we need, which is community.

The Christian faith, in its invitation to life in the Spirit, is also an invitation to life in the community of the Spirit. And that community, 'the church', is not an abstract community, but a concrete one. It is a particular set of relationships. In this chapter, we want to introduce you to life in this community.

The holy catholic church

From the very beginning, Christians have understood that faith in Jesus entails membership of his people, belonging to a community. In the words of the creed, Christians believe in the holy catholic church, the communion of saints.

What does it mean to "believe in" the church? The existence of churches is an empirical fact. To believe that there are such things as churches isn't so hard. But to believe *in* the church? What exactly does that mean? To cheer it on, like believing in the Collingwood Football Club? Let's see if we can break it down.

In the creed, the word 'catholic' means something like 'universal', 'shared', 'unified in diversity', or 'orthodox'. In modern English, the word sometimes causes confusion because it can appear to refer to the Roman Catholic Church. But any other word struggles to handle the weight-bearing load of the word 'catholic'. What's a word that means 'orthodox', and 'unity-in-diversity', and 'locally varied', and 'Christians across time and space', and 'trinitarian'? Better, we think, to use the word that says all that, and then explain what the 'all' actually includes.

What does it mean to say the church is 'catholic'? It's easier to grasp by considering the negative alternatives. A church that was not 'catholic' would be a sectarian church—fiercely independent, reluctant to acknowledge other churches as genuine, cherishing the notion that what they believe and do is exclusive to them, and taking some delight that (to paraphrase the Fleetwood Mac song) they have 'gone their own way' on some key doctrines.

By contrast, a 'catholic' church is a church that cheerfully and joyfully acknowledges that the best things about it are not unique to it. As Paul reminds the New Testament church in Corinth, these are churches who are glad to recall that they are connected "together with all those everywhere who call upon the name of the Lord" (1 Corinthians 1:2). To be a Christian is to be connected with the most multicultural and diverse people group in the history of humanity.

Church and churching

The word 'church' in the New Testament refers not to a building, but to the gathering, the assembly, the coming together of God's people. In English, we make a distinction with the definite article. If I ask you to meet me at "the church", you'll be looking for a building. If I drop the article and ask to meet you "at church", you'll be looking for an event at which Christians gather, which may or may not imply the use of a church building.

The New Testament overwhelmingly uses the word 'church' to mean a gathering of people, an assembly of believers. It is something Christians do. They 'church'. They meet together.

Question: Why do Christians church? Historically, one might argue, they had no choice. It was the only way they could achieve many important functions. Very few owned a Bible, and even those who did were unlikely to be able to read it. So gathering to hear Scripture read was essential. Not many were educated, so they gathered to hear teaching. Not many owned musical instruments, so singing and making music to God was by necessity a group effort. There were no telephones, so sharing prayer points and knowing each other's needs required real-time conversation.

Which is all to say they gathered to perform an often folksy and half-baked version of the things your smartphone could do in an instant.

The smartphone in your pocket could deliver each of those functions better than almost any congregation in history. YouTube for the world's best Christian teachers; Spotify for streaming the praise music of your choice; sharing prayer points and knowing each other's needs—there's literally an app for that.[n]

So, then, why do Christians still church?

Answer: Christians gather to be the church with actual other people. These actual bodies. These specific humans. We gather to cash out our love for the church in general with an actual love for these people in this church in particular.

In short, we gather to deliberately sacrifice some of our freedom in order to achieve community.

We believe in the church. And we believe that what happens in church is almost impossibly brilliant and beautiful. We believe that Christ is present, that his Spirit is with us, that God is addressing us in his word. We believe that our voices join with angels and archangels in heavenly praise. That we enact and participate in the never-ending

n   It's called PrayerMate.

worship of God that is currently being offered in heaven. That our words and songs please God as they are offered by the Son and through the Spirit. That we strike terror into the hearts of the evil forces. That Satan and his minions are revealed as cowardly and pathetic before the force of our praises and our declaration of the gospel. That's what we believe is happening.

But what will you see if you show up? A bunch of broken, slightly mismatched people together bashing out a church meeting which is all too obviously the product of their collective talents and limitations. The music may or may not be to your taste. The preaching may or may not connect with you. There will be a restless toddler challenging your powers of concentration and his parents' sanity. You'll meet a needy, lonely guy who is most likely there because church is his best shot at a friendly interaction in an otherwise socially sparse existence. As a group of people, they won't always Instagram well. You won't always get All The Feels.

I (Rory) am a pastor. Running a church is kind of my job. And by the grace of God (and if I may say so myself) our church is okay. Most weeks the singing, the preaching (in my humble opinion) and the fellowship are adequate, even decent. And yet, most Sundays, I have to decide to go to church. If my criteria for church attendance was "Is this the thing I most want to do right now?", I think I'd be clocking in a 2/52 annual attendance record.

It's the same with running. I never want to go running. I hate running. I prefer burgers. If I ran based on the "This is the thing I most want to do right now" metric, the results would be grim. But I do run. It's only rarely because at that moment I want to run. I run because I want to *have* run. I want to be the person who has gone for a run. I want the results of running. And, truth be told, I do actually enjoy it, nine times out of ten, once I've overcome my initial resistance.

It's the same with church. Mostly, in the moment, I don't want to go to church. But I want to have gone to church. I want to be the person that church is forming me to be. To be and become the person that that motley crew of people are shaping me into as we both give and receive grace. Once I allow my will to override my feelings, I'm almost always glad I went.

Now, as you may have guessed, we are managing your expectations a bit here. This is about as dour an account of the actual experience of church as you're very likely to find in a Christian book. Let me hasten to add: church is actually great. Almost certainly, within travelling distance of your home there is a group of Christians who gather each week to perform an imperfect rendition of the common life they believe God has called them to. They will sing God's praises, hear God's word, confess their sins, seek God's forgiveness, and greet each other, not because they are like each other, but because they follow the same Lord as each other. Local churches are like an amateur local theatre troupe, playing out the script God wrote for them with heart and verve.

If you show up there—and I hope you find this encouraging rather than creepy—you'll be meeting a group of people who have already prayed for you. They will already have asked God to bless you, to reveal himself to you, and to show you the way to salvation. Most likely, these prayers will have been general, rather than specifically naming you. But the chances that you've been prayed for by name by a Christian you know are very high. And if you've been to a local church, I am certain someone will have said a quiet prayer for you in particular after having met you or seen you there.

If you commit your life to Jesus, it will begin with prayer. And when you first pray, it won't—if I can put it this way— be the first God's heard of you. Christians will have got in ahead of you, asking God to hear and answer your prayers. I hope you find that strangely encouraging.

The communion of saints

We also believe church is the "communion of saints". This becomes at once more prosaic and more comprehensible if we rephrase it as "the fellowship of believers".

In some traditions, the word 'saints' is applied to a sub-set of high-performance Christians. In the Bible, however, 'saints' is just a standard-issue synonym for 'Christians' or 'believers'. It means people who are 'holy' or 'set apart'. This is something that all Christians are by grace, and that most Christians aspire to become in their actual lives by putting off sin and growing in righteousness. Those who achieve a degree of holiness in their lives might be called 'saintly'. But 'saint' is a title you get from the day you start with God. It's yours for free.

'Communion' or 'fellowship' means something more than

just conviviality. If I meet you in a café, our conversation may be convivial. But it would not be 'communion'. If, however, I come around to your house on a Tuesday night, and suggest that together we buy that café, or both get jobs there, or start one ourselves, then that is what the Bible would describe as a fellowship, a communion.

'Communion' means something that we 'share in'. It's the quality of relationship that comes from sharing in something together. No doubt you'll have experienced that sort of thing. Think of the sorts of relationships you might have experienced in a team that did something hard and worthwhile together. Or the relationships that emerge from a shared grief, or a mutual love of opera, or a common project of, oh, I don't know, depositing a magical ring into the heart of a volcanic mountain. These are 'fellowships'—fellowships of suffering, communion in opera, a Fellowship of the Ring. They are relationships of shared interest. For Christians, the shared interest is the Spirit and God's kingdom. I pray to God for forgiveness. I long for his kingdom to come. I experience his Spirit at work in my life. If you do too, then we share that. What we have together is fellowship, a shared life, "the communion of saints".

Conclusion

Christianity is a team sport. It is a life we live together.

On the one hand, church lifts us up out of the particulars of time, place, ethnicity, and language. It connects us with heaven, with God, and with God's people across time and space. That is what we mean by 'catholic'.

But, paradoxically, church is also the thing that embeds us in place, that ties us to a particular group of people, in a particular time and space. Churches are formed by shared interest, communion, in the one Lord. It is here that God chiefly provides what we need to keep living for him. And in doing so, he provides something that modern Western life seems so conspicuously unable to deliver: imperfect but real community.

12

The forgiveness of sins

Bloody Sunday

On 8 November 1987, the annual Remembrance Day memorial service was being held in Enniskillen, Northern Ireland. Among the attendees were local businessman Gordon Wilson and his twenty-year-old daughter Marie. At 10:43am, the Irish Republican Army (IRA) detonated an 18-kilogram bomb in the vicinity of the service. Eleven people were killed that day, including Marie Wilson. The twelfth victim, Ronnie Wilson (no relation to Gordon or Marie), died after spending 13 years in a coma.

The bombing drew a ferocious reaction from around the world. The next day, U2 were playing a concert in Colorado and during their song 'Sunday Bloody Sunday' (a song about the ongoing conflict in Northern Ireland), Bono stopped the song to express his rage:

> And let me tell you something. I've had enough of Irish Americans who haven't been back to their country in twenty or thirty years come up to me and talk about the resistance, the revolution back home, and the glory of the revolution, and the glory of dying for the revolution. F**k the revolution! ...Where's the glory in bombing a Remembrance Day parade

of old age pensioners, their medals taken out and polished up for the day? Where's the glory in that? To leave them dying, or crippled for life, or dead under the rubble of a revolution that the majority of the people in my country don't want. No more![17]

Sadly, outrage was not the only response to this atrocity. Because the victims were all Protestant, a number of revenge attacks were carried out on Roman Catholic civilians. The next day, a Protestant university student named Adam Lambert was shot dead by the Protestant paramilitary group the UDA, who had mistaken him for a Roman Catholic.

Because of the nature of this tragedy and my (Peter's) personal connections (Ronnie Wilson was the father of my maths teacher and Adam Lambert had been a few years ahead of me at school), the Enniskillen bombing made a significant impact on me as a teenager. But it was actually the response of Gordon Wilson that affected me—and many others—the most. In a number of interviews the following day, he recounted his last moments with his daughter as they lay trapped next to each other under the rubble. In a deeply emotional state, he remembered that her last words to him were "Daddy, I love you very much". He then added: "I prayed for the bombers last night that God would forgive them".[18] In another interview, he expanded on his feelings: "I bear no ill will to anybody; nor does my wife. I prayed for them last night; sincerely. I hope I get the grace to continue to do so."[19]

Gordon Wilson's attitude of forgiveness towards his daughter's murderers deeply moved a nation that was still in shock at the atrocity carried out the day before. Gordon

Wilson was a Christian man and embodied the attitude that was exemplified by Jesus. Jesus himself had uttered similar words of stunning forgiveness: as he was being crucified—being tortured and executed as an innocent man—he prayed for his executioners, "Father, forgive them, for they do not know what they are doing" (Luke 23:34).

Forgiven and forgiving

Forgiveness is a defining characteristic of the Christian life. The New Testament is not naïve enough to assume that relationships between Christians will always be smooth. It is full of exhortations to Christians to forgive or bear with one another. Famously, in The Lord's Prayer, Jesus instructs the disciples to pray "forgive us our debts, as we also have forgiven our debtors" (Matthew 6:12), adding:

> "...if you forgive other people when they sin against you, your heavenly Father will also forgive you. But if you do not forgive others their sins, your Father will not forgive your sins." (Matthew 6:14-15)

Paul writes to the Colossians to remind them that basic Christian discipleship means they must "bear with each other and forgive one another if any of you has a grievance against someone". He then adds, "Forgive as the Lord forgave you" (Colossians 3:13). This verse, I think, unveils the power of the Christian understanding of forgiveness. It is not something Christians simply imitate (by following Jesus' example), but it is something that Christians experience. Because we have experienced forgiveness, we can and we must extend it to others.

But what does it mean for the Lord to forgive us?

In the Bible, sin is falling short of God's requirements. It is our violation of the two greatest commands: to love our neighbour and to love God (Matthew 22:37-40). Sin is to fail to love your neighbour as yourself. This is either through actively hurting them, by lying, stealing, murder and the like, or through neglecting to care for them. And sin is the failure to give God his rightful, central, place in our lives. This comprehensive understanding of our responsibility as human beings leads to the Bible's judgement that "all have sinned and fall short of" God's requirements (Romans 3:23). All, without exception.

This can be difficult to swallow. There are incredibly evil people in the world: Hitler, Stalin, Mao. But surely there are good people too? We think of humanity as a tower block and we think of a particular floor as the cut-off point below which people are 'evil' and above which people are 'basically good'. Most of us think of ourselves as at least one floor, if not quite a few floors, above the cut-off point. In other words, the criterion for 'sinner' is conveniently a criterion which does not include me. What are the chances?! Just lucky, I guess.

Relational forgiveness

I think we're all aware that we do the wrong thing at different rates and to different degrees of intensity. I (Rory) had a few years at high school in which, let's just say, my behaviour wasn't of the citizenship-award-attracting variety.

One suspension, two involuntary trips in a police car, one fight (lost), any number of detentions, and a truancy record that effectively amounted to being a part-time student. Moreover, I wasn't smart enough to work under the radar, choosing instead the black jackets, dishevelled hair, and cigarette smoking that alerted anyone at first glance to my Troubled Youth status.° Peter (ironically enough, 'Pagan Pete') made it through high school with an exemplary record. Mathematically speaking, one of us fell short of school expectations more than the other. The problem is that the Bible doesn't think mathematically, but relationally. The *who* question, rather than the *how much* question, is decisive. Consider the following:

> Sam grew up in a loving and generous family. When he turned eighteen, he decided to move away to another town. For reasons known only to him, on the day he left he sat his parents down and told them that he no longer wanted anything to do with them—no contact, no visits, no relationship at all. He was even going to change his last name to express his complete break from his family. As far as he was concerned his parents no longer existed. Sam moved to his new city and lived as a model citizen. He donated a high proportion of his earnings to charity. He became a generous and loving husband and father. He was a well-respected and upstanding member of the community.[20]

o   To my sons: If you've just read this, I realize some of it may come as a surprise. We can chat later.

So it is with us and God. We might be 'naughty' or 'bad' in conspicuous ways. Or we might point to aspects of our lives—our work ethic, our care for our families, our charitable donations, our moral standards—that are, generally speaking, well ordered and even good. But even those lives, lived in the rejection of God, render us guilty before God. For the Bible, that is the essence of sin. We might not be as bad as we could be (there are plenty of people on lower floors than us), but with respect to God we have all fallen short.

So what can be done?

The Old Testament contains within it an elaborate system of sacrifice. In that sacrificial system, an animal dies in the place of the one offering the sacrifice. The New Testament says that the death of Jesus was the one true sacrifice to which those sacrifices point. He died for us, the righteous for the unrighteous, to bring us to God. Jesus, in his death, takes on the penalty for our sins and extinguishes them in his death. This is the great exchange: he takes on our sins; we are enveloped in his righteousness. This is the heart of the forgiveness won through Christ's death.

Even on the cross itself, Jesus was offering forgiveness to those who were crucified with him. One rails at Jesus, taunting him to prove his ability to save himself. The other, however, rebukes his fellow criminal and confesses his own sins: "'Don't you fear God,' he said, 'since you are under the same sentence? We are punished justly, for we are getting what our deeds deserve. But this man has done nothing wrong'" (Luke 23:40-41).

He knows he needs forgiving, and he turns to Jesus:

"Jesus, remember me when you come into your kingdom". And Jesus replies: "Truly I tell you, today you will be with me in paradise" (Luke 23:42-43).

Jesus' forgiveness of his enemies on the cross was imitated a few years later by the first Christian martyr, Stephen. As he died, being stoned by his enemies, he cried out, "Lord, do not hold this sin against them" (Acts 7:60).

In the popular podcast *Dolly Parton's America*, Jad Abumrad tells the story of Dolly Parton's troubled relationship with country music legend Porter Wagoner. Wagoner hosted the most successful country music television show of the 1960s. A then little-known Dolly Parton was given the opportunity of a lifetime—to be his new "girl singer". Parton's talents soon began to outshine Wagoner's. Jealousy plagued a decade-long dysfunctional partnership. Parton, trapped in a contract and wearied by Wagoner's manipulations and envy-driven cruelty, eventually mustered the courage to leave. Aware that Wagoner would not listen to her, she wrote the song 'I Will Always Love You', walked into his office, sang it to him, and then walked out the door, never to return.

> Bittersweet memories
> That's all I'm taking with me
> Goodbye, please don't cry
> 'Cause we both know that I'm not
> What you need...[21]

Things got ugly. As Parton's star kept rising, Wagoner's life spiralled out of control. He drank. He toured around, defaming the character of his decade-long musical partner in a series of vitriolic interviews. He sued Parton for a million dollars for breaking contract, putting her into a crippling financial situation from which it took many years to be freed.

Eventually, of course, Parton not only cleared the debt but established herself as one of the most successful musical performers of the 20th century.

If the story ended there, it would be a story of the vindication of talent and hard work over a petty and misogynistic hater. But it doesn't end there.

After Parton eventually paid the million dollars she was sued for, in 1981 Wagoner was himself dropped by his label. He was now a pathetic figure, without income or prospects. But Dolly Parton did something extraordinary: she chose to buy his publishing company and then give it back to him, rescuing him and his children from financial ruin. Years later, as Wagoner was dying, Parton went to visit him and nurse him. She spoke words of reconciliation and forgiveness to Porter. Hers was the last voice he ever heard.

On the podcast, Abumrad is clearly moved by Parton's extraordinary forgiveness. He says to her, "I have a theory that one of the reasons that you can have the broad appeal you have into so many communities that normally hate each other is because of those acts of forgiveness. Does that vibe with you?" Dolly Parton snaps back at him without flinching: "Forgiveness?! Forgiveness is all there is."

Dolly Parton is right. If imperfect, sinful people are going to live with and show love to other sinful people, then we have no other option. Forgiveness is all there is.

Bitterness, vengeance, reprisals all feed into a cycle of self-destruction. Only forgiveness can break the cycle. It's all we have.

Forgiveness is sometimes heroic. An Egyptian TV host is left stunned when the Coptic Christian woman he is interviewing says she forgives the suicide bomber who killed her husband. "How great is this forgiveness you have!" Gordon Wilson extends forgiveness to those whose bomb took the life of his daughter. Dolly Parton financially rescues the man who sued her for a million dollars. Not every Christian will have to extend this kind of heroic forgiveness. But every Christian has been on the receiving end of the utterly heroic forgiveness of Jesus. Therefore, forgiveness is the basic stance towards others that every Christian will take. The Egyptian TV presenter spoke truth at a deeper level than he realized. We are only able to extend this kind of forgiveness when we have received such a great forgiveness ourselves. We are called, says the Bible, to forgive each other, "just as in Christ God forgave [us]" (Ephesians 4:32).

13

The resurrection of the body and the life everlasting

The two resurrections

The creed mentions resurrection twice. In the middle, it affirms that "on the third day he rose again from the dead". And it concludes with "the resurrection of the body, and the life everlasting". This is not the creed doubling down on a central doctrine (so good, they mention it twice). Nor is it a slip of the pen, the authorial error of someone who forgot the topic had already been covered. No, the first mention affirms the resurrection of the one man, Jesus, in history. The second affirms the resurrection of the body—that is, the resurrection of the dead, or everyone who dies.

The two are, of course, connected. There is a place, an underworld (see chapter 1 and chapter 7), to which dead people go. A vast community of lifeless bodies, a destination to which all of us have a one-way ticket. Jesus went there. But he did something no-one else has done—he rose from among the dead. In the very place where everyone else is laid down, he stood up.

The creed ends by affirming that God will raise us too. Jesus' resurrection was not an anomaly, but a starter pistol. Jesus has smashed through the one-way door of death. His intention is to lead us through that same smashed door, by the same means. That is what is meant by the affirmation, "I believe in the resurrection of the body".

Several questions spring to mind: What? How? When? And, also, who?

What?

Or, perhaps better punctuated, What?!

It comes as a surprise to many people (and not least many Christians) that Christianity does not only teach the immortality of the soul but also the resurrection of the body. Our hope and goal is that what happened to Jesus' body will happen to our bodies: that we will be raised to participate with God in a renewed heaven and a renewed earth.

This hope flows from the logic of the story we have been following so far. A good God made a good world and placed some of his creatures, the humans, among his creation as his image-bearers. God thought that was a good idea. He still does. What he has done in Christ and through the Spirit is intended to vindicate that plan, not set it aside. And it is this: that our bodies will be raised anew, into a new creation, in which we will glorify God and enjoy him forever by being his image-bearers in his creation.

How?

The next question is: How? Human bodies, as the Bible freely acknowledges, return to the soil that sustains their lives. Apart from the very recently deceased or cryogenically frozen, what, exactly, will be raised?

The New Testament, it so happens, addresses this very question. In Paul's first letter to the Corinthians, he says that the relationship between our mortal bodies and our resurrected bodies will be like the relationship between a seed and a plant. A seed, like a body, is planted into the ground. But why is it buried? Not in order to get rid of it, but in order that it might become the very thing it was always meant to become.

The seed-and-plant picture is a picture of both discontinuity and continuity. Discontinuity: plants really are radically different things from seeds. And continuity: the plant is the realization of the seed, the fulfilment of the seed's promise. So it will be with the resurrection of our bodies. We have no idea what we will look like, or the precise mechanism that will go into the resurrection. But, somehow, we will have bodies. And they will be these bodies transformed. These bodies renewed and made into the full realization of all they were meant to be.

In this, the Christian attitude to death is transformed. From the perspective of this world, burial is a waste-disposal strategy. It is what we do with rubbish, with family pets, and with our loved ones. In the latter case, we do so respectfully, with heavy hearts, and with every dignity we can afford the deceased. But we are, as the traditional funeral service puts it, "disposing reverently of their earthly remains".

But the resurrection of Jesus holds out an alternative hope—the hope that a burial can be less like a waste-disposal ceremony and more like the planting of a new garden.

Imagine an alien visiting our world. She comes to do

some research, and she observes our waste-management strategies. We bury stuff. With this in mind, she visits a farm, and there observes the farmer burying tiny little round things into the ground. There is a plough that digs up the ground, creating these tiny graves. And into those graves the farmer drops a seed, and then he covers over the seed with dirt. What will our alien friend conclude? She will think the farmer is in the waste-management business. Clearly the farmer's job is to get rid of these small round items. The farmer's paddock is in fact a vast cemetery, and the farmer a serial killer. (Or cereal killer. Thanks, I'll let myself out.)

But the farmer is not a killer, the paddock is not a graveyard, and the job is not waste disposal. It may look like a cemetery; it is in fact a life-field. The farmer does not sow in despair, but in hope that the seeds will rise transformed. And in the resurrection of Jesus, it is as if the first of the crop has already shot up out of the ground; the firstfruits are already on the tree. The harvest awaits.[p]

When?

The timetable of when the resurrection of the dead will occur is not given to us. As far as we know, it could be next

---

p   This might raise the question of cremation, rather than burial, of the dead. It is true that Christians, along with Jews and Muslims, have tended to practise burial rather than cremation, and that this is based on a somewhat shared understanding of the nature of bodies and a belief in some sort of future resurrection. But the practice of burial is a sign and symbol of this hope, not a necessary precondition for it. To the precise "How will God raise the dead?" question, the Bible's answer is essentially, "Don't worry about it. God will sort it out". See 1 Corinthians 15:35-57.

year, or it could be thousands of years from now. The New Testament does not give us a timetable. But it does give us a sense of eager anticipation, because it will be the culmination of a process that has already started. Just as the firstfruits imply the coming harvest, the crack in the wall of the dam means the dam will soon burst, and the labour pains mean the baby is on its way, so the resurrection of Jesus means the process that will climax in resurrection has already begun.

Who?

There's a technical point and a personal point to be made here. I (Rory) will address the technical point first, then the personal. Partly because it makes sense to approach it that way, and partly because I've been avoiding writing the personal paragraph for a while now. I figure I can kick it down the road for a couple more paragraphs.

The technical question is: Who is raised? When the creed declares the resurrection of the body, is it affirming the belief that each and every human being will experience resurrection, or is it affirming that only those who believe in Jesus will be raised? I am not myself sure which the creed has in mind.

Sometimes, the New Testament affirms the resurrection of all people. Paul, for example, explicitly affirms his belief in "a resurrection of both the righteous and the wicked" (Acts 24:15). We will all stand before the judgement seat of God, and apparently we will do so in bodies, not as naked souls. So, in one sense, we will all be raised.

But the New Testament also uses resurrection language for something that is particular to the followers of Jesus. It is the hope of those who are in Christ that our bodies will be transformed to be like his glorious body (Philippians 3:21). We will be raised so as to be with our Lord (1 Thessalonians 4:13-18).

My best guess for putting it together is this: as God's image-bearers, we will all stand before him for judgement. To be human is to have a body. So, to stand before God involves standing before him in our bodies. We will be present to our maker, afforded the final dignity of an in-person audience with God, whether we followed Jesus or not. This is the general resurrection of us all.

But there is a final resurrection that is shorthand for 'resurrection to new life in the new creation under King Jesus for those who are his subjects'. Both are resurrections secured by Jesus. But only one is the kind of resurrection given to those who will spend eternity gladly under the rule and care of Jesus as his willing subjects. The other is not.

The choice we all face

Which brings me to this paragraph I've been putting off for most of this book.

Not everyone lives forever with God. The Bible, and particularly Jesus, teaches that we all face one of two futures, two options, two outcomes. It's either life with Jesus in a new creation, or life apart from God and under his judgement. This, I think, has been implicit (and occasionally explicit) in this book so far. But here I want to make it personal. If everyone faces one of those two futures, then *you* will face one of those two futures. Do you know which it will be? There is a whole discussion we could have in good faith about potentially exceptional circumstances. What about those who have never heard of God's coming judgement and the message of Jesus? Or what about babies who die before they've had a chance to respond to God? Or people in other, exceptional circumstances? In each case, I'd want to point to the goodness and justice of God, and freely admit that final judgement is well above our paygrade and competencies. We simply entrust the hard cases to the one who judges justly.

But what about you? If you have read this far, then there's a choice for you to make. Like it or not, you're now no longer in the 'I had no idea' camp. One choice would be to ignore it all and move on, like a patient ignoring a serious diagnosis from their doctor (bad decision). Or you could say you need more time, more information, more discussion. That would be a better decision, with the caveat that we can sometimes fool ourselves into thinking we need more discussion, information, or time, when what we are really doing is choosing the first option in a way we can live with.

Or it is entirely possible that based on what you know, you could make the decision to follow Jesus right now. We (that is, you and I) are also in the creed. We are among its cast of characters, along with God, Jesus, the Holy Spirit, Mary and Pilate. We are captured in the pronoun 'I'. And we are invited to do one thing, and one thing only: believe. "I believe" is the part assigned to us.

Gloriously, Christianity isn't a story about what must be done, but what has been done. It is not the story of our path to God, but of God's path to us. It is God who created, God who sent his Son, God who forgave our sins and bought us new life, and God who by his Spirit enables us to live for him. We are invited simply to believe. To believe is to trust, to entrust ourselves to the God who both made us and redeemed us.

Believing is not the ability to accept as true things that are highly unlikely, or for which there is no evidence. That is to be gullible, and to be gullible is a state against which the Bible warns, not something it praises.[q]

To say "I believe" is to say "I trust". I hand my life over to this God, I make sense of my life in this story, trusting this Saviour, empowered by this Spirit. It is to acknowledge that we have fallen short of God. That we have sinned. That we need his forgiveness. And it is to take God at his word, trusting that Jesus' death has paid the price for that sin.

I believe, and amen

The last word in the creed is the word 'Amen'. It means something like 'true' or 'yes' or 'true-and-I-am-personally-invested-in-this-truth'. Our sincere hope and prayer is that you will one day join us in looking over the words of the creed and saying, with a full heart and clear eyes, "I believe, and amen".

---

q   For warnings in the Bible against being gullible, see Mark 13:5, 1 Thessalonians 5:21, and 1 John 4:1.

ENDNOTES

1   J Kelly-Linden, 'Pandemic prompts surge in interest in prayer, Google data show', *The Telegraph*, 22 May 2020, accessed 15 August 2021. telegraph.co.uk/global-health/climate-and-people/pandemic-prompts-surge-interest-prayer-google-data-show

2   The Late Show with Stephen Colbert, 'Ricky Gervais and Stephen Go Head-to-Head on Religion' [video], *The Late Show with Stephen Colbert*, YouTube, 2 February 2017, accessed 15 August 2021. youtube.com/watch?v=P5ZOwNK6n9U

3   L Krauss, *A Universe from Nothing: Why There Is Something Rather than Nothing*, Atria, 2012.

4   NT Wright, *Simply Christian*, SPCK, 2006, p. 50.

5   R Jenson, *Systematic Theology*, vol. 1: *The Triune God*, OUP, 1997, p. 63.

6   GK Chesterton, *Orthodoxy*, House of Stratus, 2001, p. 41.

7   Quoted in Justin Taylor, '"Jesus of the Scars"', *The Gospel Coalition*, 14 July 2009, accessed 21 August 2021. thegospelcoalition.org/blogs/justin-taylor/jesus-of-scars/

8   K Barth, *Church Dogmatics*, vol. 1, *The Doctrine of the Word of God*, part 2, trans. GT Thompson and H Knight, ed. GW Bromiley and TF Torrance, T&T Clark, 1956, p. 181.

9   J Hick, *The Metaphor of God Incarnate: Christology in a Pluralistic Age*, Westminster/John Knox Press, 1993, p. ix.

10 I Glass (presenter), 'Kid Logic 2016' [radio program transcript], episode 605, *This American Life*, WBEZ, New York, 16 December 2016, accessed 25 August 2021. Included here with the kind permission of Jack Hitt. thisamericanlife.org/605/transcript

11 See B Myers, *The Apostles' Creed*, Lexham Press, 2018, p. 41.

12 This is my paraphrase of part of DL Sayers, *The Man Born to Be King: The Life of Christ in Twelve Dramatic Episodes*, Harper & Brothers, 1943, p. 304.

13 K Barth, *Dogmatics in Outline*, SCM, 1959, p. 117.

14 Myers, p. 41.

15 For CS Lewis on Christianity as "true myth", see A McGrath, *CS Lewis— A Life: Eccentric Genius, Reluctant Poet*, Tyndale House, 2016, pp. 146-151.

16 Wright, p. 3.

17 This performance of the song was featured in P Joanou, *U2: Rattle and Hum* [documentary], Paramount, United States, 1988.

18 ITN (Independent Television News), 'Ulster: Enniskillen IRA bomb' [video], *ITN*, Getty Images, 9 November 1987, accessed 15 August 2021. gettyimages.com.au/detail/video/enniskillen-ira-bomb-northern-ireland-ulster-enniskillen-news-footage/866652622

19 Religion & Ethics NewsWeekly, 'Irish Reconciliation' [video], *PBS*, PBS website, 13 June 2013, accessed 15 August 2021. pbs.org/video/religion-and-ethics-newsweekly-irish-reconciliation

20 This is an expansion of an illustration that I first heard from my (Peter's) friend Nigel Beynon.

21 D Parton, 'I Will Always Love You' [song], *Joelene*, RCA Victor, 1974.

✦matthiasmedia

Matthias Media is an independent Christian publishing company based in Sydney, Australia. To find out more information about our resources, and to access samples and free downloads, visit our website:

www.matthiasmedia.com

How to buy our resources

1. Direct from us over the internet:
   - in the US: www.matthiasmedia.com
   - in Australia: www.matthiasmedia.com.au

2. Direct from us by phone: please visit our website for current phone contact information.

3. Through a range of outlets in various parts of the world. Visit **www.matthiasmedia.com/contact** for details about recommended retailers in your part of the world.

4. Trade enquiries can be addressed to:
   - in the US and Canada: sales@matthiasmedia.com
   - in Australia and the rest of the world: sales@matthiasmedia.com.au